The Civil Disobedience Handbook

A Brief History and Practical Advice for the Politically Disenchanted

James Tracy
Editor

Manic D Press
San Francisco

Dedicated to Milton "Uncle Bud" Hendrick

Shout outs to Mission Agenda, MAC, Coalition on Homelessness SF, Mailk Rahim, the fighting tenants of North Beach and Valencia Gardens, Poor magazine, George Tirado, Hexterminators, Upski, John Nichols, Joe and Becca Geira, Aimee Patten, St. Peters Housing Committee, Homes Not Jails, Third Eye Movement, Eviction Defense Network alumni, Peter Plate, Sister Bernie Galvin, Chana Morgenstern, Richard Marquez, Randy Shaw, Brad Paul, Molotov Mouths, Allison Lum, Ted Gullicksen, Louise Vaughn, Sarah Menefee, and all of the justice seekers, elders, newcomers and dreamers. You are the ones who "Make the road by walking it," so be patient with each other. Thank you to social justice attorneys John Viola and Kim Malcheski, the Ruckus Society, and everyone who provided invaluable information and experience to this book. Thank you to Juliette Torrez for love and support.

Disclaimer: This book is for informational purposes only. No accuracy of the information herein is implied or stated. Use this information at your own risk.

Cover by Scott Idleman/BLINK.

Library of Congress Cataloging-in-Publication Data

The civil disobedience handbook : a brief history and practical advice for the politically disenchanted / edited by James Tracy.
    p. cm.
Includes bibliographical references.
  ISBN 0-916397-76-9 (pbk)
  1. Civil disobedience—United States. 2. Civil rights—United States. I. Tracy, James.
  JC328.3 .C544 2002
  322.4'0973—dc21

                  2002003691

Eternal vigilance is the price of liberty!
— *Jacob A. Riis, 'The Making of an American'*

"Let us not seek to satisfy our thirst for freedom by drinking from the cup of bitterness and hatred. We must forever conduct our struggle on the high plane of dignity and discipline. We must not allow our creative protest to degenerate into physical violence. Again and again we must rise to the majestic heights of meeting physical force with soul force." — *Dr. Martin Luther King, Jr.*

CONTENTS

Why Dissent Still Matters

In 1849, when Henry David Thoreau wrote, "That government is best which governs least," his words became a memorable part of the pre-Civil War, anti-slavery upheaval. His essays popularized the idea of civil disobedience against injustice. The Labor Movement, the Women's Movement, the Civil Rights Movement, and the '60s Peace Movement used civil disobedience to force the federal government to change our laws and end the Vietnam War. Civil disobedience has recently been very effective in drawing media attention to environmental issues and in the continuing recent triumphs of the worldwide anti-globalization movement.

A lot has changed in America since 1849; unfortunately much has stayed the same. Thoreau reinforced the notion that dissent was natural, rational, desirable, and even a patriotic duty. He saw civil disobedience as a form of governance in and of itself, and was deeply dubious of elections, perhaps foreseeing the 2000 Florida presidential election debacle by a century and a half.

Although the events of September 11, 2001 have instilled an almost McCarthyite political conformity throughout this country, dissent still matters in the United States. It matters if you are a minimum wage worker considering organizing your workplace. It matters if you are the high school student threatened with expulsion for wearing an anti-war t-shirt to school. It matters if the destruction of the Alaskan wilderness bothers you in any way. Dissent matters to the millions of people locked up in prison for non-violent offenses and a generation of youth being ushered into that system. It matters if your housing project is close to a toxic superfund site, or if your suburban house is downwind from an oil refinery. Dissent certainly matters if your retirement benefits have been stolen by your corporation's CEO. And dissent really matters if you don't like your personal freedom and unalienable rights to Life, Liberty, and the pursuit of Happiness taken away by the federal government.

Dissent matters if you think the War on Terrorism is starting to look a lot like almost every other war before it. If dissent didn't matter anymore then John Ashcroft wouldn't have had to push through the USA PATRIOT Act that may not do much to stop terrorism, but will be used to stifle protest movements through increased surveillance and wiretap powers. The rhetoric from Washington D.C. is that every American must "fight to preserve freedom." I couldn't agree more.

As John Sellers from the Ruckus Society so aptly put it: "We need to communicate with and inspire people. We have to be vigilant to not be marginalized and inspire people in the center to join us."

Dear reader, this book is for you.

BILL OF RIGHTS
The first 10 amendments to the US Constitution, ratified on December 15, 1791

The Conventions of a number of the States having, at the time of adopting the Constitution, expressed a desire, in order to prevent misconstruction or abuse of its powers, that further declaratory and restrictive clauses should be added, and as extending the ground of public confidence in the Government will best insure the beneficent ends of its institution;

Resolved, by the Senate and House of Representatives of the United States of America, in Congress assembled, two-thirds of both Houses concurring, that the following articles be proposed to the Legislatures of the several States, as amendments to the Constitution of the United States; all or any of which articles, when ratified by three-fourths of the said Legislatures, to be valid to all intents and purposes as part of the said Constitution, namely:

Amendment I - Congress shall make no law respecting an establishment of religion, or prohibiting the free exercise thereof; or abridging the freedom of speech, or of the press; or the right of the people peaceably to assemble, and to petition the government for a redress of grievances.

Amendment II - A well regulated militia, being necessary to the security of a free state, the right of the people to keep and bear arms, shall not be infringed.

Amendment III - No soldier shall, in time of peace be quartered in any house, without the consent of the owner, nor in time of war, but in a manner to be prescribed by law.

Amendment IV - The right of the people to be secure in their persons, houses, papers, and effects, against unreasonable searches and seizures, shall not be violated, and no warrants shall issue, but upon probable cause, supported by oath or affirmation, and particularly describing the place to be searched, and the persons or things to be seized.

Amendment V - No person shall be held to answer for a capital, or otherwise infamous crime, unless on a presentment or indictment of a grand jury, except in cases arising in the land or naval forces, or in the militia, when in actual service in time of war or public danger; nor shall any person be subject for the same offense to be twice put in jeopardy of life or limb; nor shall be compelled in any criminal case to be a witness against himself, nor be deprived of life, liberty, or property, without due process of law; nor shall private property be taken for public use, without just compensation.

Amendment VI - In all criminal prosecutions, the accused shall enjoy the right to a speedy and public trial, by an impartial jury of the state and district wherein the crime shall have been committed, which district shall have been previously ascertained by law, and to be informed of the nature and cause of the accusation; to be confronted with the witnesses against him; to have compulsory process for obtaining witnesses in his favor, and to have the assistance of counsel for his defense.

Amendment VII - In suits at common law, where the value in controversy shall exceed twenty dollars, the right of trial by jury shall be preserved, and no fact tried by a jury, shall be otherwise reexamined in any court of the United States, than according to the rules of the common law.

Amendment VIII - Excessive bail shall not be required, nor excessive fines imposed, nor cruel and unusual punishments inflicted.

Amendment IX - The enumeration in the Constitution, of certain rights, shall not be construed to deny or disparage others retained by the people.

Amendment X - The powers not delegated to the United States by the Constitution, nor prohibited by it to the states, are reserved to the states respectively, or to the people.

The Boston Tea Party

One of the most infamous acts of American civil disobedience helped spark the Revolutionary War, and the founding of this country. In 1773, Britain's East India Company, on the verge of bankruptcy, possessed large amounts of tea that it could not sell in England. In an effort to save the company from bankruptcy, the government passed the Tea Act of 1773, which gave the company the right to export its merchandise directly to the colonies without paying any of the regular taxes that were imposed on the colonial merchants, who had traditionally served as the middlemen in such transactions. With these privileges, the company could undersell American merchants and monopolize the colonial tea trade. The colonists responded by boycotting tea. Unlike earlier protests, this boycott mobilized large segments of the population. It also helped link the colonies together in a common experience of mass popular protest. Particularly important to the movement were the activities of colonial women, who were one of the principal consumers of tea and now became the leaders of the boycott.

Various colonies made plans to prevent the East India Company from landing its cargoes in colonial ports. In ports other than Boston, agents of the company were forced to resign, and new shipments of tea were returned to England. In Boston, the agents refused to resign and, with the support of the royal governor, preparations were made to land incoming cargoes regardless of opposition. After failing to turn back the three ships in the harbor, local patriots led by Samuel Adams staged a daring action of civil disobedience. On the evening of December 16, 1773, fifty men masquerading as Mohawk Indians went aboard the three ships, broke open the tea chests, and heaved £9,659 worth of Darjeeling into the harbor. As the electrifying news of the Boston incident spread, other seaports followed the example and staged similar acts of resistance.

Of the Boston Tea Party, John Adams wrote, "There is a dignity, a majesty, a sublimity, in this last effort of the patriots that I greatly admire."

On the Duty of Civil Disobedience
by Henry David Thoreau
[1849, original title: Resistance to Civil Government]

I heartily accept the motto, "That government is best which governs least"; and I should like to see it acted up to more rapidly and systematically. Carried out, it finally amounts to this, which also I believe—"That government is best which governs not at all"; and when men are prepared for it, that will be the kind of government which the people will have. Government is at best but an expedient; but most governments are usually, and all governments are sometimes, inexpedient. The objections which have been brought against a standing army, and they are many and weighty, and deserve to prevail, may also at last be brought against a standing government. The standing army is only an arm of the standing government. The government itself, which is only the mode which the people have chosen to execute their will, is equally liable to be abused and perverted before the people can act through it. Witness the present Mexican war, the work of comparatively a few individuals using the standing government as their tool; for in the outset, the people would not have consented to this measure.

This American government—what is it but a tradition, though a recent one, endeavoring to transmit itself unimpaired to posterity, but each instant losing some of its integrity? It has not the vitality and force of a single living man; for a single man can bend it to his will. It is a sort of wooden gun to the people themselves. But it is not the less necessary for this; for the people must have some complicated machinery or other, and hear its din, to satisfy that idea of government which they have. Governments show thus how successfully men can be imposed upon, even impose on themselves, for their own advantage. It is excellent, we must all allow. Yet this government never of itself furthered any enterprise, but by the alacrity with which it got out of its way. It does not keep the country free. It does not settle the West. It does not educate. The character inherent in the American people has done all that has been accomplished; and it would have done somewhat more, if the government had not sometimes got in its way. For government is an expedient, by which men would faint succeed in letting one another alone; and, as has been said, when it is most expedient, the governed are most let alone by it. Trade and commerce, if they were not made of india-rubber, would never manage to bounce over obstacles which legislators are continually putting in their way; and if one were to judge these men wholly by the effects of their actions and not partly by their intentions, they would deserve to be classed and punished with those mischievious persons who put obstructions on the railroads.

But, to speak practically and as a citizen, unlike those who call themselves no-government men, I ask for, not at once no government, but at once a better government. Let every man make known what kind of government would command his respect, and that will be one step toward obtaining it.

After all, the practical reason why, when the power is once in the hands of the people, a majority are permitted, and for a long period continue, to rule is not because they are most likely to be in the right, nor because this seems fairest to the minority, but because they are physically the strongest. But a government in which the majority rule in all cases can not be based on justice, even as far as men understand it. Can there not be a government in which the majorities do not virtually decide right and wrong, but conscience? — in which majorities decide only those questions to which the rule of expediency is applicable? Must the citizen ever for a moment, or in the least degree, resign his conscience to the legislator? Why has every man a conscience then? I think that we should be men first, and subjects afterward. It is not desirable to cultivate a respect for the law, so much as for the right. The only obligation which I have a right to assume is to do at any time what I think right. It is truly enough said that a corporation has no conscience; but a corporation on conscientious men is a corporation with a conscience. Law never made men a whit more just; and, by means of their respect for it, even the well-disposed are daily made the agents on injustice. A common and natural result of an undue respect for the law is, that you may see a file of soldiers, colonel, captain, corporal, privates, powder-monkeys, and all, marching in admirable order over hill and dale to the wars, against their wills, ay, against their common sense and consciences, which makes it very steep marching indeed, and produces a palpitation of the heart. They have no doubt that it is a damnable business in which they are concerned; they are all peaceably inclined. Now, what are they? Men at all? or small movable forts and magazines, at the service of some unscrupulous man in power? Visit the Navy Yard, and behold a marine, such a man as an American government can make, or such as it can make a man with its black arts—a mere shadow and reminiscence of humanity, a man laid out alive and standing, and already, as one may say, buried under arms with funeral accompaniment, though it may be,

"Not a drum was heard, not a funeral note,
As his course to the rampart we hurried;
Not a soldier discharged his farewell shot
O'er the grave where our hero was buried."

The mass of men serve the state thus, not as men mainly, but as machines, with their bodies. They are the standing army, and the militia, jailers, constables, posse comitatus, etc. In most cases there is no free exercise whatever of the judgement or of the moral sense; but they put themselves on a level with wood and earth and stones; and wooden men can perhaps be manufactured that will serve the purpose as well. Such command no more respect than men of straw or a lump of dirt. They have the same sort of worth only as horses and dogs. Yet such as these even are commonly esteemed good citizens. Others—as most legislators, politicians, lawyers, ministers, and office-holders—serve the state chiefly with their heads; and, as the rarely make any moral distinctions, they are as likely to serve the devil, without intending it, as God. A very few—as heroes, patriots, martyrs, reformers in the great sense, and men—serve the state with their consciences also, and so necessarily resist it for the most part; and they are commonly treated as enemies by it. A wise man will only be useful as a man, and will not submit to be "clay," and "stop a hole to keep the wind away," but leave that office to his dust at least:

"I am too high born to be propertied,
To be a second at control,
Or useful serving-man and instrument
To any sovereign state throughout the world."

He who gives himself entirely to his fellow men appears to them useless and selfish; but he who gives himself partially to them is pronounced a benefactor and philanthropist.

How does it become a man to behave toward the American government today? I answer, that he cannot without disgrace be associated with it. I cannot for an instant recognize that political organization as my government which is the slave's government also.

All men recognize the right of revolution; that is, the right to refuse allegiance to, and to resist, the government, when its tyranny or its inefficiency are great and unendurable. But almost all say that such is not the case now. But such was the case, they think, in the Revolution of '75. If one were to tell me that this was a bad government because it taxed certain foreign commodities brought to its ports, it is most probable that I should not make an ado about it, for I can do without them. All machines have their friction; and possibly this does enough good to counter-balance the evil. At any rate, it is a great evil to make a stir about it. But when the friction comes to have its machine, and oppression and robbery are organized, I say, let us not have such a machine any longer. In other words, when a sixth of the population of a nation which has undertaken to be the refuge of liberty are slaves, and a whole country is unjustly overrun and conquered by a foreign army, and subjected to military law, I think that it is not too soon for honest men to rebel and revolutionize. What makes this duty the more urgent is that fact that the country so overrun is not our own, but ours is the invading army.

Paley, a common authority with many on moral questions, in his chapter on the "Duty of Submission to Civil Government," resolves all civil obligation into expediency; and he proceeds to say that "so long as the interest of the whole society requires it, that it, so long as the established government cannot be resisted or changed without public inconveniencey, it is the will of God... that the established government be obeyed—and no longer. This principle being admitted, the justice of every particular case of resistance is reduced to a computation of the quantity of the danger and grievance on the one side, and of the probability and expense of redressing it on the other." Of this, he says, every man shall judge for himself. But Paley appears never to have contemplated those cases to which the rule of expediency does not apply, in which a people, as well and an individual, must do justice, cost what it may. If I have unjustly wrested a plank from a drowning man, I must restore it to him though I drown myself. This, according to Paley, would be inconvenient. But he that would save his life, in such a case, shall lose it. This people must cease to hold slaves, and to make war on Mexico, though it cost them their existence as a people.

In their practice, nations agree with Paley; but does anyone think that Massachusetts does exactly what is right at the present crisis?

"A drab of stat, a cloth-o'-silver slut,
To have her train borne up, and her soul trail in the dirt."

Practically speaking, the opponents to a reform in Massachusetts are not a hundred thousand politicians at the South, but a hundred thousand merchants and farmers here, who are more interested in commerce and agriculture than they are in humanity, and are not prepared to do justice to the slave and to Mexico, cost what it may. I quarrel not with far-off foes, but with those who, neat at home, co-operate with, and do the bidding of, those far away, and without whom the latter would be harmless. We are accustomed to say, that the mass of men are unprepared; but improvement is slow, because the few are not as materially wiser or better than the many. It is not so important that many should be good as you, as that there be some absolute goodness somewhere; for that will leaven the whole lump. There are thousands who are in opinion opposed to slavery and to the war, who yet in effect do nothing to put an end to them; who, esteeming themselves children of Washington and Franklin, sit down with their hands in their pockets, and say that they know not what to do, and do nothing; who even postpone the question of freedom to the question of free trade, and quietly read the prices-current along with the latest advices from Mexico, after dinner, and, it may be, fall asleep over them both. What is the price-current of an honest man and patriot today? They hesitate, and they regret, and sometimes they petition; but they do nothing in earnest and with effect. They will wait, well disposed, for other to remedy the evil, that they may no longer have it to regret. At most, they give up only a cheap vote, and a feeble countenance and Godspeed, to the right, as it goes by them. There are nine hundred and ninety-nine patrons of virtue to one virtuous man. But it is easier to deal with the real possessor of a thing than with the temporary guardian of it.

All voting is a sort of gaming, like checkers or backgammon, with a slight moral tinge to it, a playing with right and wrong, with moral questions; and betting naturally accompanies it. The character of the voters is not staked. I cast my vote, perchance, as I think right; but I am not vitally concerned that that right should prevail. I am willing to leave it to the majority. Its obligation, therefore, never exceeds that of expediency. Even voting for the right is doing nothing for it. It is only expressing to men feebly your desire that it should prevail. A wise man will not leave the right to the mercy of chance, nor wish it to prevail through the power of the majority. There is but little virtue in the action of masses of men. When the majority shall at length vote for the abolition of slavery, it will be because they are indifferent to slavery, or because there is but little slavery left to be abolished by their vote. They will then be the only slaves. Only his vote can hasten the abolition of slavery who asserts his own freedom by his vote.

I hear of a convention to be held at Baltimore, or elsewhere, for the selection of a candidate for the Presidency, made up chiefly of editors, and men who are politicians by profession; but I think, what is it to any independent, intelligent, and respectable man what decision they may come to? Shall we not have the advantage of this wisdom and honesty, nevertheless? Can we not count upon some independent votes? Are there not many individuals in the country who do not attend conventions? But no: I find that the respectable man, so called, has immediately drifted from his position, and despairs of his country, when his country has more reasons to despair of him. He forthwith adopts one of the candidates thus selected as the only available one, thus proving that he is himself available for any purposes of the demagogue. His vote is of no more worth than that of any unprincipled foreigner or hireling native, who may have been bought. O for a man who is a man, and, and my neighbor says, has a bone is his back which you cannot pass your hand through! Our statistics are at fault: the population has been returned too large. How many men are there to a square thousand miles in the country? Hardly one. Does not America offer any inducement for men to settle here? The American has dwindled into an Odd Fellow— one who may be known by the development of his organ of gregariousness, and a manifest lack of intellect and cheerful self-reliance; whose first and chief concern, on coming into the world, is to see that the almshouses are in good repair; and, before yet he has lawfully donned the virile garb, to collect a fund to the support of the widows and orphans that may be; who, in short, ventures to live only by the aid of the Mutual Insurance company, which has promised to bury him decently.

It is not a man's duty, as a matter of course, to devote himself to the eradication of any, even to most enormous, wrong; he may still properly have other concerns to engage him; but it is his duty, at least, to wash his hands of it, and, if he gives it no thought longer, not to give it practically his support. If I devote myself to other pursuits and contemplations, I must first see, at least, that I do not pursue them sitting upon another man's shoulders. I must get off him first, that he may pursue his contemplations too. See what gross inconsistency is tolerated. I have heard some of my townsmen say, "I should like to have them order me out to help put down an insurrection of the slaves, or to march to Mexico—see if I would go"; and yet these very men have each, directly by their allegiance, and so indirectly, at least, by their money, furnished a substitute. The soldier is applauded who refuses to serve in an unjust war by those who do not refuse to sustain the unjust government which makes the war; is applauded by those whose own act and authority he disregards and sets at naught; as if the state were penitent to that degree that it hired one to scourge it while it sinned, but not to that degree that it left off sinning for a moment. Thus, under the name of Order and Civil Government, we are all made at last to pay homage to and support our own meanness. After the first blush of sin comes its indifference; and from immoral it becomes, as it were, unmoral, and not quite unnecessary to that life which we have made.

The broadest and most prevalent error requires the most disinterested virtue to sustain it. The slight reproach to which the virtue of patriotism is commonly liable, the noble are most likely to incur. Those who, while they disapprove of the character and measures of a government, yield to it their allegiance and support are undoubtedly its most conscientious supporters, and so frequently the most serious obstacles to reform. Some are petitioning the State to dissolve the Union, to disregard the requisitions of the President. Why do they not dissolve it themselves—the union between themselves and the State—and refuse to pay their quota into its treasury? Do not they stand in same relation to the State that the State does to the Union? And have not the same reasons prevented the State from resisting the Union which have prevented them from resisting the State?

How can a man be satisfied to entertain and opinion merely, and enjoy it? Is there any enjoyment in it, if his opinion is that he is aggrieved? If you are cheated out of a single dollar by your neighbor, you do not rest satisfied with knowing you are cheated, or with saying that you are cheated, or even with petitioning him to pay you your due; but you take effectual steps at once to obtain the full amount, and see to it that you are never cheated again. Action from principle, the perception and the performance of right, changes things and relations; it is essentially revolutionary, and does not consist wholly with anything which was. It not only divided States and churches, it divides families; ay, it divides the individual, separating the diabolical in him from the divine.

Unjust laws exist: shall we be content to obey them, or shall we endeavor to amend them, and obey them until we have succeeded, or shall we transgress them at once? Men, generally, under such a government as this, think that they ought to wait until they have persuaded the majority to alter them. They think that, if they should resist, the remedy would be worse than the evil. But it is the fault of the government itself that the remedy is worse than the evil. It makes it worse. Why is it not more apt to anticipate and provide for reform? Why does it not cherish its wise minority? Why does it cry and resist before it is hurt? Why does it not encourage its citizens to put out its faults, and do better than it would have them? Why does it always crucify Christ and excommunicate Copernicus and Luther, and pronounce Washington and Franklin rebels?

One would think, that a deliberate and practical denial of its authority was the only offense never contemplated by its government; else, why has it not assigned its definite, its suitable and proportionate, penalty? If a man who has no property refuses but once to earn nine shillings for the State, he is put in prison for a period unlimited by any law that I know, and determined only by the discretion of those who put him there; but if he should steal ninety times nine shillings from the State, he is soon permitted to go at large again.

If the injustice is part of the necessary friction of the machine of government, let it go, let it go: perchance it will wear smooth— certainly the machine will wear out. If the injustice has a spring, or a pulley, or a rope, or a crank, exclusively for itself, then perhaps you may consider whether the remedy will not be worse than the evil; but if it is of such a nature that it requires you to be the agent of injustice to another, then I say, break the law. Let your life be a counter-friction to stop the machine. What I have to do is to see, at any rate, that I do not lend myself to the wrong which I condemn.

As for adopting the ways of the State has provided for remedying the evil, I know not of such ways. They take too much time, and a man's life will be gone. I have other affairs to attend to. I came into this world, not chiefly to make this a good place to live in, but to live in it, be it good or bad. A man has not everything to do, but something; and because he cannot do everything, it is not necessary that he should be petitioning the Governor or the Legislature any more than it is theirs to petition me; and if they should not hear my petition, what should I do then? But in this case the State has provided no way: its very Constitution is the evil. This may seem to be harsh and stubborn and unconcilliatory; but it is to treat with the utmost kindness and consideration the only spirit that can appreciate or deserves it. So is all change for the better, like birth and death, which convulse the body.

I do not hesitate to say, that those who call themselves Abolitionists should at once effectually withdraw their support, both in person and property, from the government of Massachusetts, and not wait till they constitute a majority of one, before they suffer the right to prevail through them. I think that it is enough if they have God on their side, without waiting for that other one. Moreover, any man more right than his neighbors constitutes a majority of one already.

I meet this American government, or its representative, the State government, directly, and face to face, once a year—no more—in the person of its tax-gatherer; this is the only mode in which a man situated as I am necessarily meets it; and it then says distinctly, Recognize me; and the simplest, the most effectual, and, in the present posture of affairs, the indispensablest mode of treating with it on this head, of expressing your little satisfaction with and love for it, is to deny it then. My civil neighbor, the tax-gatherer, is the very man I have to deal with— for it is, after all, with men and not with parchment that I quarrel—and he has voluntarily chosen to be an agent of the government. How shall he ever know well that he is and does as an officer of the government, or as a man, until he is obliged to consider whether he will treat me, his neighbor, for whom he has respect, as a neighbor and well-disposed man, or as a maniac and disturber of the peace, and see if he can get over this obstruction to his neighborlines without a ruder and more impetuous thought or speech corresponding with his action. I know this well, that if one thousand, if one hundred, if ten men whom I could name—if ten honest men only—ay, if one HONEST man, in this State of Massachusetts, ceasing to hold slaves, were actually to withdraw from this co-partnership, and be locked up in the county jail therefor, it would be the abolition of slavery in America. For it matters not how small the beginning may seem to be: what is once well done is done forever. But we love better to talk about it: that we say is our mission. Reform keeps many scores of newspapers in its service, but not one man. If my esteemed neighbor, the State's ambassador, who will devote his days to the settlement of the question of human rights in the Council Chamber, instead of being threatened with the prisons of Carolina, were to sit down the prisoner of Massachusetts, that State which is so anxious to foist the sin of slavery upon her sister—though at present she can discover only an act of inhospitality to be the ground of a quarrel with her—the Legislature would not wholly waive the subject of the following winter.

Under a government which imprisons unjustly, the true place for a just man is also a prison. The proper place today, the only place which Massachusetts has provided for her freer and less despondent spirits, is in her prisons, to be put out and locked out of the State by her own act, as they have already put themselves out by their principles. It is there that the fugitive slave, and the Mexican prisoner on parole, and the Indian come to plead the wrongs of his race should find them; on that separate but more free and honorable ground, where the State places those who are not with her, but against her—the only house in a slave State in which a free man can abide with honor. If any think that their influence would be lost there, and their voices no longer afflict the ear of the State, that they would not be as an enemy within its walls, they do not know by how much truth is stronger than error, nor how much more eloquently and effectively he can combat injustice who has experienced a little in his own person. Cast your whole vote, not a strip of paper merely, but your whole influence. A minority is powerless while it conforms to the majority; it is not even a minority then; but it is irresistible when it clogs by its whole weight. If the alternative is to keep all just men in prison, or give up war and slavery, the State will not hesitate which to choose. If a thousand men were not to pay their tax bills this year, that would not be a violent and bloody measure, as it would be to pay them, and enable the State to commit violence and shed innocent blood. This is, in fact, the definition of a peaceable revolution, if any such is possible. If the tax-gatherer, or any other public officer, asks me, as one has done, "But what shall I do?" my answer is, "If you really wish to do anything, resign your office." When the subject has refused allegiance, and the officer has resigned from office, then the revolution is accomplished. But even suppose blood shed when the conscience is wounded? Through this wound a man's real manhood and immortality flow out, and he bleeds to an everlasting death. I see this blood flowing now.

I have contemplated the imprisonment of the offender, rather than the seizure of his goods—though both will serve the same purpose—because they who assert the purest right, and consequently are most dangerous to a corrupt State, commonly have not spent much time in accumulating property. To such the State renders comparatively small service, and a slight tax is wont to appear exorbitant, particularly if they are obliged to earn it by special labor with their hands. If there were one who lived wholly without the use of money, the State itself would hesitate to demand it of him. But the rich man—not to make any invidious comparison—is always sold to the institution which makes him rich. Absolutely speaking, the more money, the less virtue; for money comes between a man and his objects, and obtains them for him; it was certainly no great virtue to obtain it. It puts to rest many questions which he would otherwise be taxed to answer; while the only new question which it puts is the hard but superfluous one, how to spend it. Thus his moral ground is taken from under his feet. The opportunities of living are diminished in proportion as that are called the "means" are increased. The best thing a man can do for his culture when he is rich is to endeavor to carry out those schemes which he entertained when he was poor. Christ answered the Herodians according to their condition. "Show me the tribute-money," said he—and one took a penny out of his pocket—if you use money which has the image of Caesar on it, and which he has made current and valuable, that is, if you are men of the State, and gladly enjoy the advantages of Caesar's government, then pay him back some of his own when he demands it. "Render therefore to Caesar that which is Caesar's and to God those things which are God's"—leaving them no wiser than before as to which was which; for they did not wish to know.

When I converse with the freest of my neighbors, I perceive that, whatever they may say about the magnitude and seriousness of the question, and their regard for the public tranquillity, the long and the short of the matter is, that they cannot spare the protection of the existing government, and they dread the consequences to their property and families of disobedience to it. For my own part, I should not like to think that I ever rely on the protection of the State. But, if I deny the authority of the State when it presents its tax bill, it will soon take and waste all my property, and so harass me and my children without end. This is hard. This makes it impossible for a man to live honestly, and at the same time comfortably, in outward respects. It will not be worth the while to accumulate property; that would be sure to go again. You must hire or squat somewhere, and raise but a small crop, and eat that soon. You must live within yourself, and depend upon yourself always tucked up and ready for a start, and not have many affairs. A man may grow rich in Turkey even, if he will be in all respects a good subject of the Turkish government. Confucius said: "If a state is governed by the principles of reason, poverty and misery are subjects of shame; if a state is not governed by the principles of reason, riches and honors are subjects of shame." No: until I want the protection of Massachusetts to be extended to me in some distant Southern port, where my liberty is endangered, or until I am bent solely on building up an estate at home by peaceful enterprise, I can afford to refuse allegiance to Massachusetts, and her right to my property and life. It costs me less in every sense to incur the penalty of disobedience to the State than it would to obey. I should feel as if I were worth less in that case.

Some years ago, the State met me in behalf of the Church, and commanded me to pay a certain sum toward the support of a clergyman whose preaching my father attended, but never I myself. "Pay," it said, "or be locked up in the jail." I declined to pay. But, unfortunately, another man saw fit to pay it. I did not see why the schoolmaster should be taxed to support the priest, and not the priest the schoolmaster; for I was not the State's schoolmaster, but I supported myself by voluntary subscription. I did not see why the lyceum should not present its tax bill, and have the State to back its demand, as well as the Church. However, as the request of the selectmen, I condescended to make some such statement as this in writing: "Know all men by these presents, that I, Henry Thoreau, do not wish to be regarded as a member of any society which I have not joined." This I gave to the town clerk; and he has it. The State, having thus learned that I did not wish to be regarded as a member of that church, has never made a like demand on me since; though it said that it must adhere to its original presumption that time. If I had known how to name them, I should then have signed off in detail from all the societies which I never signed on to; but I did not know where to find such a complete list.

I have paid no poll tax for six years. I was put into a jail once on this account, for one night; and, as I stood considering the walls of solid stone, two or three feet thick, the door of wood and iron, a foot thick, and the iron grating which strained the light, I could not help being struck with the foolishness of that institution which treated me as if I were mere flesh and blood and bones, to be locked up. I wondered that it should have concluded at length that this was the best use it could put me to, and had never thought to avail itself of my services in some way. I saw that, if there was a wall of stone between me and my townsmen, there was a still more difficult one to climb or break through before they could get to be as free as I was. I did not for a moment feel confined, and the walls seemed a great waste of stone and mortar. I felt as if I alone of all my townsmen had paid my tax. They plainly did not know how to treat me, but behaved like persons who are underbred. In every threat and in every compliment there was a blunder; for they thought that my chief desire was to stand the other side of that stone wall. I could not but smile to see how industriously they locked the door on my meditations, which followed them out again without let or hindrance, and they were really all that was dangerous. As they could not reach me, they had resolved to punish my body; just as boys, if they cannot come at some person against whom they have a spite, will abuse his dog. I saw that the State was half-witted, that it was timid as a lone woman with her silver spoons, and that it did not know its friends from its foes, and I lost all my remaining respect for it, and pitied it.

Thus the state never intentionally confronts a man's sense, intellectual or moral, but only his body, his senses. It is not armed with superior with or honesty, but with superior physical strength. I was not born to be forced. I will breathe after my own fashion. Let us see who is the strongest. What force has a multitude? They only can force me who obey a higher law than I. They force me to become like themselves. I do not hear of men being forced to live this way or that by masses of men. What sort of life were that to live? When I meet a government which says to me, "Your money or your life," why should I be in haste to give it my money? It may be in a great strait, and not know what to do: I cannot help that. It must help itself; do as I do. It is not worth the while to snivel about it. I am not responsible for the successful working of the machinery of society. I am not the son of the engineer. I perceive that, when an acorn and a chestnut fall side by side, the one does not remain inert to make way for the other, but both obey their own laws, and spring and grow and flourish as best they can, till one, perchance, overshadows and destroys the other. If a plant cannot live according to nature, it dies; and so a man.

The night in prison was novel and interesting enough. The prisoners in their shirtsleeves were enjoying a chat and the evening air in the doorway, when I entered. But the jailer said,

"Come, boys, it is time to lock up"; and so they dispersed, and I heard the sound of their steps returning into the hollow apartments. My room-mate was introduced to me by the jailer as "a first-rate fellow and clever man." When the door was locked, he showed me where to hang my hat, and how he managed matters there. The rooms were whitewashed once a month; and this one, at least, was the whitest, most simply furnished, and probably neatest apartment in town. He naturally wanted to know where I came from, and what brought me there; and, when I had told him, I asked him in my turn how he came there, presuming him to be an honest man, of course; and as the world goes, I believe he was. "Why," said he, "they accuse me of burning a barn; but I never did it." As near as I could discover, he had probably gone to bed in a barn when drunk, and smoked his pipe there; and so a barn was burnt. He had the reputation of being a clever man, had been there some three months waiting for his trial to come on, and would have to wait as much longer; but he was quite domesticated and contented, since he got his board for nothing, and thought that he was well treated.

He occupied one window, and I the other; and I saw that if one stayed there long, his principal business would be to look out the window. I had soon read all the tracts that were left there, and examined where former prisoners had broken out, and where a grate had been sawed off, and heard the history of the various occupants of that room; for I found that even there there was a history and a gossip which never circulated beyond the walls of the jail. Probably this is the only house in the town where verses are composed, which are afterward printed in a circular form, but not published. I was shown quite a long list of young men who had been detected in an attempt to escape, who avenged themselves by singing them.

I pumped my fellow-prisoner as dry as I could, for fear I should never see him again; but at length he showed me which was my bed, and left me to blow out the lamp.

It was like travelling into a far country, such as I had never expected to behold, to lie there for one night. It seemed to me that I never had heard the town clock strike before, not the evening sounds of the village; for we slept with the windows open, which were inside the grating. It was to see my native village in the light of the Middle Ages, and our Concord was turned into a Rhine stream, and visions of knights and castles passed before me. They were the voices of old burghers that I heard in the streets. I was an involuntary spectator and auditor of whatever was done and said in the kitchen of the adjacent village inn—a wholly new and rare experience to me. It was a closer view of my native town. I was fairly inside of it. I never had seen its institutions before.

This is one of its peculiar institutions; for it is a shire town. I began to comprehend what its inhabitants were about.

In the morning, our breakfasts were put through the hole in the door, in small oblong-square tin pans, made to fit, and holding a pint of chocolate, with brown bread, and an iron spoon. When they called for the vessels again, I was green enough to return what bread I had left, but my comrade seized it, and said that I should lay that up for lunch or dinner. Soon after he was let out to work at haying in a neighboring field, whither he went every day, and would not be back till noon; so he bade me good day, saying that he doubted if he should see me again.

When I came out of prison—for some one interfered, and paid that tax—I did not perceive that great changes had taken place on the common, such as he observed who went in a youth and emerged a gray-headed man; and yet a change had come to my eyes come over the scene—the town, and State, and country, greater than any that mere time could effect. I saw yet more distinctly the State in which I lived. I saw to what extent the people among whom I lived could be trusted as good neighbors and friends; that their friendship was for summer weather only; that they did not greatly propose to do right; that they were a distinct race from me by their prejudices and superstitions, as the Chinamen and Malays are that in their sacrifices to humanity they ran no risks, not even to their property; that after all they were not so noble but they treated the thief as he had treated them, and hoped, by a certain outward observance and a few prayers, and by walking in a particular straight through useless path from time to time, to save their souls. This may be to judge my neighbors harshly; for I believe that many of them are not aware that they have such an institution as the jail in their village.

It was formerly the custom in our village, when a poor debtor came out of jail, for his acquaintances to salute him, looking through their fingers, which were crossed to represent the jail window, "How do ye do?" My neighbors did not this salute me, but first looked at me, and then at one another, as if I had returned from a long journey. I was put into jail as I was going to the shoemaker's to get a shoe which was mended. When I was let out the next morning, I proceeded to finish my errand, and, having put on my mended shoe, joined a huckleberry party, who were impatient to put themselves under my conduct; and in half an hour—for the horse was soon tackled—was in the midst of a huckleberry field, on one of our highest hills, two miles off, and then the State was nowhere to be seen.

This is the whole history of "My Prisons."

I have never declined paying the highway tax, because I am as desirous of being a good neighbor as I am of being a bad subject;

and as for supporting schools, I am doing my part to educate my fellow countrymen now. It is for no particular item in the tax bill that I refuse to pay it. I simply wish to refuse allegiance to the State, to withdraw and stand aloof from it effectually. I do not care to trace the course of my dollar, if I could, till it buys a man a musket to shoot one with—the dollar is innocent—but I am concerned to trace the effects of my allegiance. In fact, I quietly declare war with the State, after my fashion, though I will still make use and get what advantages of her I can, as is usual in such cases.

If others pay the tax which is demanded of me, from a sympathy with the State, they do but what they have already done in their own case, or rather they abet injustice to a greater extent than the State requires. If they pay the tax from a mistaken interest in the individual taxed, to save his property, or prevent his going to jail, it is because they have not considered wisely how far they let their private feelings interfere with the public good.

This, then is my position at present. But one cannot be too much on his guard in such a case, lest his actions be biased by obstinacy or an undue regard for the opinions of men. Let him see that he does only what belongs to himself and to the hour.

I think sometimes, Why, this people mean well, they are only ignorant; they would do better if they knew how: why give your neighbors this pain to treat you as they are not inclined to? But I think again, This is no reason why I should do as they do, or permit others to suffer much greater pain of a different kind. Again, I sometimes say to myself, When many millions of men, without heat, without ill will, without personal feelings of any kind, demand of you a few shillings only, without the possibility, such is their constitution, of retracting or altering their present demand, and without the possibility, on your side, of appeal to any other millions, why expose yourself to this overwhelming brute force? You do not resist cold and hunger, the winds and the waves, thus obstinately; you quietly submit to a thousand similar necessities. You do not put your head into the fire. But just in proportion as I regard this as not wholly a brute force, but partly a human force, and consider that I have relations to those millions as to so many millions of men, and not of mere brute or inanimate things, I see that appeal is possible, first and instantaneously, from them to the Maker of them, and, secondly, from them to themselves. But if I put my head deliberately into the fire, there is no appeal to fire or to the Maker for fire, and I have only myself to blame. If I could convince myself that I have any right to be satisfied with men as they are, and to treat them accordingly, and not according, in some respects, to my requisitions and expectations of what they and I ought to be, then, like a good Mussulman and fatalist, I should endeavor to be satisfied with things as they are, and say it is the will of God. And, above all, there is this difference between resisting this and a purely brute or natural force, that I can resist this with some effect; but I cannot expect, like Orpheus, to change the nature of the rocks and trees and beasts.

I do not wish to quarrel with any man or nation. I do not wish to split hairs, to make fine distinctions, or set myself up as better than my neighbors. I seek rather, I may say, even an excuse for conforming to the laws of the land. I am but too ready to conform to them. Indeed, I have reason to suspect myself on this head; and each year, as the tax-gatherer comes round, I find myself disposed to review the acts and position of the general and State governments, and the spirit of the people to discover a pretext for conformity.

"We must affect our country as our parents,
And if at any time we alienate
Out love or industry from doing it honor,
We must respect effects and teach the soul
Matter of conscience and religion,
And not desire of rule or benefit."

I believe that the State will soon be able to take all my work of this sort out of my hands, and then I shall be no better patriot than my fellow-countrymen. Seen from a lower point of view, the Constitution, with all its faults, is very good; the law and the courts are very respectable; even this State and this American government are, in many respects, very admirable, and rare things, to be thankful for, such as a great many have described them; seen from a higher still, and the highest, who shall say what they are, or that they are worth looking at or thinking of at all?

However, the government does not concern me much, and I shall bestow the fewest possible thoughts on it. It is not many moments that I live under a government, even in this world. If a man is thought-free, fancy-free, imagination-free, that which is not never for a long time appearing to be to him, unwise rulers or reformers cannot fatally interrupt him.

I know that most men think differently from myself; but those whose lives are by profession devoted to the study of these or kindred subjects content me as little as any. Statesmen and legislators, standing so completely within the institution, never distinctly and nakedly behold it. They speak of moving society, but have no resting-place without it. They may be men of a certain experience and discrimination, and have no doubt invented ingenious and even useful systems, for which we sincerely thank them; but all their wit and usefulness lie within certain not very wide limits. They are wont to forget that the world is not governed by policy and expediency. Webster never goes behind government, and so cannot speak with authority about it. His words are wisdom to those legislators who contemplate no essential reform in the existing government; but for thinkers, and those who legislate for all time, he never once glances at the subject. I know of those whose serene and wise speculations on this theme would soon reveal the limits of his mind's range and hospitality. Yet, compared with the cheap professions of most reformers, and the still cheaper wisdom an eloquence of politicians in general, his are almost the only sensible and valuable words, and we thank Heaven for him. Comparatively, he is always strong, original, and, above all, practical. Still, his quality is not wisdom, but prudence. The lawyer's truth is not Truth, but consistency or a consistent expediency. Truth is always in harmony with herself, and is not concerned chiefly to reveal the justice that may consist with wrong-doing. He well deserves to be called, as he has been called, the Defender of the Constitution. There are really no blows to be given him but defensive ones. He is not a leader, but a follower. His leaders are the men of '87. "I have never made an effort," he says, "and never propose to make an effort; I have never countenanced an effort, and never mean to countenance an effort, to disturb the arrangement as originally made, by which various States came into the Union." Still thinking of the sanction which the Constitution gives to slavery, he says, "Because it was part of the original compact—let it stand." Notwithstanding his special acuteness and ability, he is unable to take a fact out of its merely political relations, and behold it as it lies absolutely to be disposed of by the intellect—what, for instance, it behooves a man to do here in American today with regard to slavery—but ventures, or is driven, to make some such desperate answer to the following, while professing to speak absolutely, and as a private man—from which what new and singular of social duties might be inferred? "The manner," says he, "in which the governments of the States where slavery exists are to regulate it is for their own consideration, under the responsibility to their constituents, to the general laws of propriety, humanity, and justice, and to God. Associations formed elsewhere, springing from a feeling of humanity, or any other cause, have nothing whatever to do with it. They have never received any encouragement from me and they never will. [These extracts have been inserted since the lecture was read -HDT]

They who know of no purer sources of truth, who have traced up its stream no higher, stand, and wisely stand, by the Bible and the Constitution, and drink at it there with reverence and humanity; but they who behold where it comes trickling into this lake or that pool, gird up their loins once more, and continue their pilgrimage toward its fountainhead.

No man with a genius for legislation has appeared in America. They are rare in the history of the world. There are orators, politicians, and eloquent men, by the thousand; but the speaker has not yet opened his mouth to speak who is capable of settling the much-vexed questions of the day. We love eloquence for its own sake, and not for any truth which it may utter, or any heroism it may inspire. Our legislators have not yet learned the comparative value of free trade and of freed, of union, and of rectitude, to a nation. They have no genius or talent for comparatively humble questions of taxation and finance, commerce and manufactures and agriculture. If we were left solely to the wordy wit of legislators in Congress for our guidance, uncorrected by the seasonable experience and the effectual complaints of the people, America would not long retain her rank among the nations. For eighteen hundred years, though perchance I have no right to say it, the New Testament has been written; yet where is the legislator who has wisdom and practical talent enough to avail himself of the light which it sheds on the science of legislation.

The authority of government, even such as I am willing to submit to—for I will cheerfully obey those who know and can do better than I, and in many things even those who neither know nor can do so well—is still an impure one: to be strictly just, it must have the sanction and consent of the governed. It can have no pure right over my person and property but what I concede to it. The progress from an absolute to a limited monarchy, from a limited monarchy to a democracy, is a progress toward a true respect for the individual. Even the Chinese philosopher was wise enough to regard the individual as the basis of the empire. Is a democracy, such as we know it, the last improvement possible in government? Is it not possible to take a step further towards recognizing and organizing the rights of man? There will never be a really free and enlightened State until the State comes to recognize the individual as a higher and independent power, from which all its own power and authority are derived, and treats him accordingly. I please myself with imagining a State at last which can afford to be just to all men, and to treat the individual with respect as a neighbor; which even would not think it inconsistent with its own repose if a few were to live aloof from it, not meddling with it, nor embraced by it, who fulfilled all the duties of neighbors and fellow men. A State which bore this kind of fruit, and suffered it to drop off as fast as it ripened, would prepare the way for a still more perfect and glorious State, which I have also imagined, but not yet anywhere seen.

Women are People, Too: The Suffragettes

Although the movement for women's right to vote evolved in the late 19th century (out of women's activism in and frustration with the anti-slavery movement), the first mass demonstrations for suffrage weren't held until 1911. They were organized by suffragist leader Alice Paul, who had been impressed by the militancy of the British suffrage movement while she was traveling in England.

A suffrage parade in 1913 on the eve of President Wilson's inauguration was marred by violence, but also helped to integrate the movement. Members of the black sorority Delta Sigma Theta marched as a delegation, while black journalist and anti-lynching activist Ida B. Wells marched side-by-side with white women from Illinois.

In 1916 and 1917 suffragists picketed the White House, with one silent picket leading to the arrest of 218 women from 26 states. The 19th amendment guaranteeing women the right to vote passed Congress in 1919 and was ratified in 1920.

The Folks Who Brought You the Weekend: The Labor Movement

The 1930s were a pivotal time for working-class direct action. The International Union of All Workers used disruptive tactics to occupy Hormel slaughterhouses and force contract negotiations. Similar to the earlier influential Industrial Workers of the World, the IUAW relied on work slowdowns, sit-down strikes and road shutdowns to regulate corporate abuse.

The union also organized outside of the meat packing industry. Affiliated women workers shut down a Woolworth's store in protest of poor wages, foreshadowing the Civil Rights desegregation efforts by three decades.

In the view of many labor activists, a traditional strike might be the least effective of actions because a strike can allow the employer to replace workers under current labor laws. When President Reagan fired striking air-traffic controllers without remorse in August 1981, he set a precedent that has weakened unions ever since.

The contemporary Industrial Workers of the World provides the following suggestions for today's militant workers:

Slowdowns - Workers stay on the job but drag production to a halt. Slowdowns are often a part of a work-to-rule effort.

Work-To-Rule - Disgruntled workers may break rules in order to achieve a little bit of workplace justice. Don't forget that following the rules can be a form of direct action. Employers often encourage workers to cut corners in order to save time and money. During one labor dispute at a post office, workers actually checked every single package in order to ensure proper postage. It's hard to fire someone when they are following the rules exactly.

Sit-down Strikes - Effective for a variety of reasons. Like walkouts, they cost the boss a lot of money. Since the workers stay in the factory, employers were less likely to resort to violence for fear of harm befalling their equipment.

Good Work Strike - Such a strike aims to build solidarity between workers who provide a good or service and those who receive it. For example, bus drivers battling for better wages can let riders on the bus for free. Angry cafe workers can give out free coffee. Nurses in one hospital stayed on the job because a strike would harm patients and turn the public against the union, instead they simply "forgot" to fill out billing papers or charge for prescriptions.

Sick In - These actions are especially effective when employees are forbidden to strike because of a law or a labor agreement. All employees at a work place calling in sick on the same day can basically shut down a business altogether. Workers can stay at home or meet and organize for the next action.

Recently, through acts of civil disobedience, minimum wage workers and student activists at Harvard University, the nation's richest school, won an impressive set of demands from the campus administration. The changes raised janitorial and cafeteria workers' salaries by nearly 100% thanks in part to a twenty-one day occupation of the President's office in 2001.

The Harvard Living Wage Campaign had attempted to gain pay and benefit concessions for low-wage workers, and found that the key to its success was a worker-student alliance willing to risk arrest for a just cause.

The office occupation helped to galvanize an even broader base of support for the workers, and solidarity rallies often brought out 1,500 people. Activists seized on the fact that Harvard enjoyed a $20 million endowment but paid some workers minimum wage. The workers' unions, Hotel and Restaurant Workers Local 21 and Service Employees International Union Local 254, hope that this victory will inspire more unusual alliances such as this and put a fighting face on the labor movement once more. The workers insisted on not accepting any settlement that would leave open the possibility that students would be reprimanded for their solidarity. Similar actions have occurred at University of Michigan, University of Iowa, University of Wisconsin, and Wesleyan.

I Have A Dream: The Civil Rights Movement

In 1955, Rosa Parks, a 43-year-old black seamstress and trained activist, was arrested in Montgomery, Alabama, for refusing to give up her seat on a bus to a white man. The following night, fifty leaders of the black community met at Dexter Ave. Baptist Church to discuss the issue. Among them was a young minister, Dr. Martin Luther King, Jr. The leaders organized the Montgomery Bus Boycott, which deprived the bus company of 65% of its income, and cost Dr. King a $500 fine or 386 days in jail. He paid the fine, and eight months later, the Supreme Court decided that, based on the 1954 Brown v. Board of Education decision that segregation was unconstitutional, bus segregation violated the constitution.

On February 1, 1960 the first student sit-in for desegregation took place in Greensboro, North Carolina. Four students from the North Carolina Agricultural and Technical College carried out the action. Joseph McNeill, David Richmond, Izell Blair and Franklin McCain walked into a Woolworth's store, bought a few things, then sat at the lunch counter reserved for whites. They attracted little attention, were not served, and remained there until closing.

The students returned the next day with thirty others and made headlines. On the third day, nearly all of the seats reserved for whites were occupied by black students. The confrontations, which included the now-famous images of whites emptying sugar canisters on the heads of the protesters and a bomb threat, forced the temporary closing of the store. Similar sit-ins spread across the state quickly. Concord, Elizabeth City, High Point, Fayetteville, Charlotte, Raleigh, Durham and Winston-Salem became sit-in sites in the next two weeks.

More dramatic were the Freedom Rides of 1961. Southern Jim Crow practices separated black from white in all aspects of interstate bus travel. The mode of civil disobedience was simple: civil rights workers would take the same busses across states and deliberately ignore segregation wherever they might encounter it — bathrooms, waiting areas or ticket purchase lines. Although the Supreme Court had ruled in 1947 that segregation during interstate travel was illegal, the ruling applied only to seating arrangements en route and not to any other areas of the bus stations. Racist violence met the students nearly every step of the way. One bus was set on fire. Freedom riders were often beaten as they disembarked. The riders adhered to the tactic of nonviolence and refused to strike back.

In 1963, black men and women in Birmingham, Alabama held sit-ins at lunch counters where they were refused service, and "kneel-ins" on church steps where they were denied entrance, one of the most severely segregated cities in America. Hundreds of demonstrators were fined and imprisoned. In 1963, Dr. King, the Reverend Abernathy and the Reverend Shuttlesworth led a protest march in Birmingham. The protestors were met with policemen and dogs. The three ministers were arrested and taken to Southside Jail.

In 1965, the black community of Marion, Alabama decided to hold a march to protest the killing of a demonstrator by a state trooper. Martin Luther King agreed to lead the marchers on Sunday, March 7, from Selma to Montgomery, the state capital, where they would appeal directly to Governor Wallace to stop police brutality and call attention to their struggle for suffrage. When Governor Wallace refused to allow the march, Dr. King went to Washington to speak with President Johnson, delaying the demonstration until March 8. However, the people of Selma could not wait and they began the march on Sunday. When the marchers reached the city line, they found a large squad of state troopers waiting for them. As the demonstrators crossed the bridge leading out of Selma, they were ordered to disperse, but the troopers did not wait for their warning to be heeded. They immediately attacked the crowd of people who had bowed their heads in prayer. Using tear gas and batons, the troopers chased the demonstrators to a black housing project, where they continued to beat the demonstrators as well as residents of the project who had not been at the march.

This terrible event received national attention, and numerous marches were organized in response. Martin Luther King led a march to the Selma bridge that Tuesday, during which one protestor was killed. Finally, with President Johnson's permission, Dr. King led a successful march from Selma to Montgomery on March 25. President Johnson gave a rousing speech to Congress concerning civil rights as a result of these events, and the Voting Rights Act was passed within that same year.

The Student Nonviolent Coordinating Committee (SNCC), founded in 1960, was mostly comprised of college-age activists. SNCC's involvement with the civil rights movement demonstrated that a civil disobedience campaign must have some kind of sustained economic disruption if it is to achieve lasting reforms. The lunch-counter occupations and the freedom rides organized by SNCC directly threatened the profits of major corporations. SNCC's campaign created a strategic chaos of sustained business disruption. SNCC believed that activists from the black community were key to the struggle, but did not shy away from white participants.

Implicit in this strategy was the effort to make the South as ungovernable for authorities as it had been unlivable for blacks. In one sense, transforming the everyday bigoted violence into explicitly political forms created the type of crisis that the government had to respond to. This kind of mass civil disobedience, aimed at making fundamental change in society, is always a risk. Through forcing the government to take action, there is always the real possibility that the action taken will be more violence. The freedom riders wagered that such a crisis would pit local and federal governments against each other and that the federal government would ultimately respond through instituting meaningful reforms.

To an extent they were successful. President Kennedy at that point provided protection through a helicopter escort, but inexplicably withdrew it, setting up the students for arrest. In the upper South, desegregation of bus terminals was successful, but in the deep South the facilities would remain segregated for quite some time to come.

The actions of SNCC and the larger Civil Rights movement unleashed an era of dissent and upheaval that would influence many other movements such as the anti-war movement and third-world liberation movements.

Civil Rights Movement veteran Alma Lark witnessed many acts of civil disobedience and spent time in between many of the organizations of the time, including the SCLC and SNCC. She saw the need for a movement to be rooted in the everyday work of office operations and fundraising in order to provide an adequate foundation for disruptive action. "There were a lot of us who were the power behind the action. I took up the task of fundraising for the movement, which was necessary because we were taking so many risks, and there were so many arrests. It was wonderful to be a part of such history."

Lark remains proud of the gains of the movement — especially school desegregation. "When the President finally signed the Civil Rights legislation, I knew that it took a movement of people in order to bring his hand to that piece of paper. It was such rough going to get to that point, and it has been rough going since."

Now a grandmother, Lark still leads by example when she implores young people to stay involved in the fight for social justice. She has been active in her tenant association at North Beach Public Housing. "Young people must be diligent and sincere if they hope to achieve anything. Every generation must renew the struggle, but those of us who have been around for awhile cannot leave it either.

"I listen to people today, and I know that there is still discontent and a yearning for justice. But people are not organized like they were before and they have to get organized."

Peace Now: The Anti–Vietnam War Movement

During the four years following passage of the Tonkin Gulf resolution in 1964, which authorized U.S. military action in Southeast Asia, the American air war intensified and troop levels climbed to over 500,000. Opposition to the war grew as television and press coverage graphically showed the suffering of both civilians and soldiers.

In 1965, demonstrations in New York City attracted 25,000 marchers; within two years similar demonstrations drew several hundred thousand participants in Washington, D.C., London, and other European capitals. Most of the demonstrations were peaceful, though acts of civil disobedience were common. Much of the impetus for the anti-war protests came from college students. Objections to the military draft led some protesters to burn their draft cards and to refuse to obey induction notices.

In 1968 the Students for a Democratic Society (SDS) sponsored a demonstration at Columbia University that ended in the arrest of more than 700 protesters. That same year, President Johnson, who was challenged by two anti-war candidates within his own party for the presidential nomination, Senators Eugene McCarthy and Robert Kennedy, chose not to run. The Democratic Convention in Chicago that year was wracked by acts of civil disobedience. The election of Richard Nixon in 1968 and his reduction in U.S. ground forces did little to dampen the anti-war movement. His decision to invade Cambodia in 1970 led to massive demonstrations on college campuses, most tragically at Kent State University where four people were killed by members of the Ohio National Guard. A massive march on Washington in 1971 comprised of students, housewives, union members, veterans, and many others shut down the entire East Coast for a day, and finally the end of the war in Vietnam began.

Richard Nixon finally admitted, "Although publicly I continued to ignore the raging anti-war controversy ... I knew, however, that after all the protests and the Moratorium [the nationwide protests of October 1969], American public opinion would be seriously divided by any military escalation of the war."

From Activist to Officer: One Cop's Story

When it comes to the politics of protest, Sergeant Kevin Paulson has been on both sides of the barricade. As a member of ACT-UP New York, he participated in dramatic actions that shut down the Brooklyn Bridge, the Stock Exchange, pharmaceutical companies, the federal Food and Drug Administration (FDA) and many branches of the local government as well.

Like many activists, Paulson had been around protest politics for awhile before being moved into more confrontational tactics. He founded the first coming out group at the University of Michigan which, according to Paulson, "seemed like a revolutionary act at the time, given the climate."

Paulson's commitment was intensified watching the spread of the fatal epidemic, the utter indifference of public officials, and drug company profiteering. "ACT-UP was successful in so many ways, but if we had gotten started in 1982 instead of 1987 many lives would have been saved." Some of the accomplishments of ACT-UP were forcing the FDA into Parallel Track Testing, so that multiple parts of a drug trail could be done at once, funding for research, and programs to support people struggling with the virus.

"In 1987, my best friend had just came out positive. New York had only 54 beds allotted for people with AIDS. Some guy on the Health Commission said that only about 1% of New York's population was gay - only about 300,000." This invisibility directly translated into inaction on all levels of government in the face of an epidemic.

That commissioner awoke one morning to find handprints in red paint leading from City Hall to his house. "We showed that blood was on his hands. ACT-UP was phenomenal, we were so organized. We broke into three main committees: Information, that did all of the research; Media, in charge of the counter-spin; and Actions. I joined the actions committee since I didn't have any other skills, really. We had the advantage of having advertising people and doctors join us in the fight and they were often put into the first two committees."

Paulson stresses that the main goal of ACT-UP's action committee should be shared by other CD activists as well. "Have focus and bring attention to the issue. So many actions these days don't have any focus and they don't bring much attention to the cause at all. You can't reach everyone, but you can put the case out there and force people in power to pay attention. There is always a response/counter-response. There would always be some people who are pissed off that there are a bunch of angry fags protesting. There are others who will wake up and realize that we wouldn't be protesting if we didn't have a situation that needed action.

"Our actions always had multiple roles: the arrestees, the media liaisons, the legal team, the police liaisons, and those who showed up to make the crowd big. You could not be arrested unless you were trained in CD. We taught every aspect of what to expect and what to do. We gave hints on how to be handcuffed — cross your wrists so the officer can't cut off your circulation with the cuffs."

As an ACT-UP member Paulson grew aware that the problems facing the nation in terms of social justice were larger than his issue. "We were doing a blockade, nine white men and one black. The cops dragged the black guy out of the line and beat him up while yelling 'Don't resist! Don't resist!' It was then I realized it still could be a crime to be black in America, or gay for that matter."

Today Paulson has traded in his Silence=Death t-shirts for the uniform of the San Francisco Sheriff's Department. He is in charge of most of the security for City Hall, and now attends protests as the arrestor not the arrestee. While this might seem as blasphemy to some, Paulson offers a very convincing case for the transformation.

"We were having a gigantic kiss-in when the play *Larry Kramer Kissed Me* opened in New York. A kiss-in is where hundreds of gays would just kiss in public places for visibility — that was HOT! I lived in Jersey City, New Jersey. After the action I took the train home, and was confronted by a group of teenagers who couldn't stand the t-shirt I was wearing: a picture of two men kissing with the caption 'Read My Lips'. I was beaten up badly."

The next day, Paulson went to the police station to file a report, wearing the bloodied t-shirt. The police officer in charge refused to take the report and bluntly stated, "I'm so sick of having to protect faggots." When Paulson retorted that he was entitled to the same protections as anyone else, the officer replied that "no faggot could do or understand" his job.

Paulson set out to prove him wrong. He moved to San Francisco and became a cop. "San Francisco is a pretty liberal city — but I'm challenging homophobia and discrimination in institutions most resistant to change: the police. It's my form of activism now."

Among San Francisco's activists, Paulson has a reputation for professionalism. Many seasoned protesters have been surprised to be treated so well by an officer of the law. "I tell my people to treat protesters with respect, no matter what the cause is. This is part of their human rights to advocate for their beliefs. Play by the book. I have been known to write up officers who manhandle protesters."

ACT-UP left a permanent impression on Paulson's life. "We put a face on the epidemic, that was a proud one. When George Bush, Sr. said he was going to fund programs for the 'undeserving victims' of the epidemic we knew he meant 'straight victims.' We sent a message that we are your brothers, sisters, sons, and children."

Defending A Woman's Right To Choose

In 1973, the Supreme Court decided in Roe vs. Wade that women have the right, by virtue of freedom of privacy, to choose if and when to terminate their pregnancies. Since then, the war over women's bodies has raged in the streets, in Congress, and at the ballot box. The Christian Right has used the right-to-choose issue to expand influence within the Republican Party and push an agenda that limits women's freedom.

Just how effective has the anti-choice movement been? The Feminist Majority Foundation conducted a survey of harassment of clinics that provided abortion during the years 1992-1997 and made the following findings: Severe violence plagued about 25% of clinics; staff resignations as a result of anti-abortion violence and harassment went up; and vandalism and bomb threats at women's health facilities were the most common forms of violence in 1997. Just under 60% of the clinics experienced some form of picketing at their facilities at the time of data collection. It is ironic that the Right Wing has been successful in building a movement by co-opting much of the tactics and rhetoric of the Civil Rights era — minus the emphasis on non-violence.

When anti-abortion groups attempt to shut down women's health clinics, all sorts of distinctions are blurred and roles are temporarily reversed. It is the right wing that is engaged in civil disobedience, and various women's and community groups are there to prevent a blockade. From minute to minute, it is unclear where the police stand. Sometimes they act to keep the clinic open by arresting anti-choice blockaders; at other times, they refuse to enforce the law and randomly lash out at the pro-choice demonstrators protecting the clinic.

A typical Clinic Defense goes something like this: the pro-choice demonstrators link arms and attempt to secure an unbreakable path for women to pass through unharmed to the clinic. Anti-choice demonstrators try to break the human barrier so they can blockade the building and prevent women from having abortions that day. The anti-choice demonstrators attempt to harass and intimidate women who are already emotionally vulnerable. Pro-choice clinic defenders escort each woman safely into the building.

Susan Jones fought from behind her enemy's line in this war. As a young pro-choice student attending an East Coast university, she participated first in clinic defense and later worked as an infiltrator inside the anti-choice movement. As an infiltrator, she gathered information and disseminated it to pro-choice organizations in the area, giving them advance notice of which clinics were to be targeted, and where and when anti-choice actions were to take place.

Jones's strategy was to begin slowly, visiting and later joining the group Ivy League Right To Lifers that operated a Birthright Pregnancy Crisis Center. "I went in posing as a pregnant woman and met with a mother/daughter team of counselors. I thought they would start off with the typical gory dead baby pictures, but they didn't. These women took the approach 'you are so far from home, you must be so afraid.'

"I really thought that the right was segmented into the people who were actually attacking clinics and the pregnancy crisis counseling people. But they were very entwined. What freaked me out was that it was the same people at every event. The same people who were at Birthright or Ivy Leaguers for Life meetings were at the Operation Rescue rallies shutting down clinics," Jones explained. "A man would come up to me at a meeting and say, 'See that guy over there? He's with the Lambs of Christ. Do you know who the Lambs of Christ are?' I would say, 'Well, yes, I do, that's the paramilitary group,' and would think that I never really thought I would encounter them."

Jones eventually left this form of activism because of the burnout associated with living one's life as a secret agent. "Two years is a long time to spend being someone that you're not. After that point I moved. I was trained to infiltrate by a longtime pro-choice activist. She didn't infiltrate as much but she put other people in. She studied the connections between the KKK and the anti-choice movement. When you are infiltrating it's not as if you don't ever get caught up in their rhetoric, as a matter of fact you do. I would call home every four hours and have a friend remind me what I was doing."

The present threat to a woman's right to make decisions about her body is extremely alarming. President Bush recently reiterated his anti-choice views at a conservative Christian rally, and U.S. Attorney General John Ashcroft is decidedly in favor of a constitutional amendment outlawing abortion. Ashcroft told a conservative newsletter in 1998, "If I had the opportunity to pass but a single law, I would... ban every abortion except for those medically necessary to save the life of the mother."

Jones believes that civil disobedience actions will be an important tool for social and economic justice organizers. "I think civil disobedience will be a vital tactic in the coming years. You can talk and talk but at some point we'll have to put it on the line. Living in these Bush years is like a flashback to when I was infiltrating. I hear what comes out of his mouth and think it's all coming back around again."

The Art of Social Justice

Many social movements have employed expressive arts as an organizing tool. During the Great Depression labor union organizers would use participatory theater to educate illiterate workers about rights and resistance. Billie Holiday's anti-lynching song "Strange Fruit" was mailed to every member of Congress by supporters of anti-lynching legislation. During the 1960s Teatro Campesino was an integral part of farm worker organizing while the San Francisco Mime Troupe brought its brand of free political satire to parks and other social spaces.

In the late 1990s there was a resurgence of using art, poetry and music as protest tools. Not only have demonstrations become beautiful to look at, with giant puppets and creative props, but artists were actually using their art to take over urban spaces, commit civil disobedience, and make public political statements. David Solnit of Art and Revolution said, "When we were in Toronto last year for the IMF Summit, one activist group was down on the ideas of art and puppets, and Californians in general. We won them over when they realized that we were serious about using art to occupy space and thereby making it harder for authorities to break up the demonstration."

Multi-disciplined creator Praba Pilar has always mixed art with political actions. Born in New York City to Columbian parents, she moved throughout Latin America as a child. "Since I moved a lot I saw a lot of different social structures, a lot of different ways of being. I knew early on that there is some choice in the social contract. Also, I became a bit of an outsider and an observer."

An anti-racist perspective fuels most of Pilar's work. In 1995, she worked with the United Farm Workers to recreate a roadside strawberry stand inside an art gallery. The installation supported UFW's "Five Cents For Fairness" campaign in which growers were asked to spend a nickel for every basket sold to improve wages for farm workers. The installation featured videos of workers, employers, politicians, and activists commenting on the campaign.

Pilar's career can be described as a perpetual rebellion against the tyranny she witnessed throughout the Americas. She also credits heavy dosages of punk rock as a youth in forming a confrontational aesthetic. A college stint majoring in Third World Studies helped her understand the enormity of the structures she wished to challenge. "I also went to work for ACORN doing tenant organizing in New York City. Low-income tenants were fighting to get vacant buildings turned over for a dollar to community groups. The civil disobedience they practiced was intense because they had so much more to lose than professional organizers. Ultimately they won, and it was exhilarating.

"I'm not content just to make pieces about causes, I'm the type of artist that gets into the action." Wherever there is action against injustice, count on Pilar to be there. "One of my most memorable acts of civil disobedience was in New York City, in protest of the 1983 U.S. invasion of Grenada. We shut down the CIA building with 300 people. We blockaded the entrances and no one got in or out. The police brought in horses. They were trained to use the animals to break the blockade, to make people scatter as the horses stood on hind legs and thrust their front hooves through the activists linking arms around the building. However, we had been trained on how not to run but separate just enough to allow the horses to land in between us. This allowed us to hold the barricade for a very long time."

Pilar was reminded of that action when she attended the protests against the World Trade Center Organization's 1999 conference in Seattle. "What worked in Seattle was that the tactics were multi-layered. You had celebrity activists inside the conference. The lockdown in the middle of the streets was so effective. The art was beautiful and strategically placed. The Secretary of State couldn't leave her hotel room. That's real and concrete — we shut it down!" Pilar takes a lot of inspiration from the wave of protests that have sprung up since the Seattle 1999 protest. Her work, in part, is to keep the momentum and optimism of that time going.

Currently Pilar works with the Hexterminators, a group that combines performance art and confrontational political action. She believes that art is an integral part of struggle. "Art is the cultural front of struggle. You can't have a revolution without revolutionary culture."

The Hexterminators reach people on different levels. "We use very strange visuals to shock people into conversation through guerilla theater. We want to get under the radar and start a conversation through our guerilla theater." The group has dressed in business clothing in order to broaden their appeal at actions.

Pilar has an optimistic and independent vision for movement building in the future. "We prove that you don't need funding or non-profit status to work on an issue. What we do is very public and we do it whether or not there is funding to do so. Our direct actions have been broadcast all over the globe raising the issue of where our planet is going. Every action must have a web and a radio component, to make the impact last beyond its site. The web is used for self-publishing so that experiences can be archived and analyzed."

The Hexterminators also advocate Culture Jamming as a tactic for spreading awareness of an issue. Culture Jamming is a technique when an icon of dominant culture is taken and "reappropriated" to convey a critical message. For example, Pilar's group once placed warnings about bio-engineered food into the format of discount coupons for those products and distributed them at shopping centers. "There are a lot of good resources for culture jammers but the best stuff is always generated locally by people who know what their community will respond to."

Her advice for young activists is, "Always look great when you are getting busted. At one action, I was sick and my ribs were bruised but I smiled as I was getting arrested to tell them you just can't keep a good woman down."

She also warns that art and politics are entwined, not separate work. "You can' t have a political art movement without straight-up political organizing. I learned everything I know from door-knocking with ACORN."

Housing Takeovers

As the nation's cities become filled with more and more homeless people and that population becomes filled with more and more families, many homeless activists have taken to the tactic takeovers of vacant housing in order to organize, educate and house human beings in need.

In many cities, the federal government is the largest holder of such properties. Throughout the 1990s, Religious Witness With Homeless People, led by Sister Bernie Galvin, challenged such federal acts of exclusion. They set their sights upon housing at the Presidio, a decommissioned Army base in San Francisco. Thousands of units of decent housing sat vacant against a green and pristine view of the Pacific Ocean. Religious Witness had to face down a federal plan to privatize the area and lease it off to for-profit developers.

Throughout the multi-year campaign, hundreds of clergy people were arrested occupying housing. Although none of the targeted housing was ever turned over, many speculated that it was the pressure of this campaign that convinced the Feds to include transitional housing for homeless veterans on the site.

In Washington D.C. there are over 29,000 buildings classified as abandoned compared to about 14,000 homeless people. Homes Not Jails DC continues to lead the fight to use these buildings for low-income people. "This simply is not the way we are meant to live in the world," remarked Lisa Davis of HNJ. HNJ has a good track record of success using a simple methodology: 1) Work with a core group of dedicated people, including people experiencing poverty, to scout out vacant buildings. 2) Research the properties at the Public Recorder or Assessor's office. Such information such as tax delinquency is public record. 3) Visit the site beforehand, and look for structural soundness. Are there holes in the floor? Are the joists secure? 4) Look for buildings where the owner is out-of-town. If they can't be contacted, they can't press charges. Often, in the federal government, it is difficult to locate the official who has power to press charges, extending the stay of the occupiers. 5) There are two kinds of takeovers: those used to make a political point and those used to house people covertly for the long-term. If you are considering occupying a house, you should know the difference. Even when takeovers have been symbolic, participating homeless people have reaped some concessions from the local government. "All of the homeless people who have participated in the actions have gotten housing of some sort," concluded Davis. "Our city officials get pretty embarrassed when we point out in the press that we as people are doing what they, as the government, should be doing."

The Whole World Was Watching: Seattle 99

November 30, 1999 renewed the call for mass protest and raised a lot of awareness around the issues and dangers of economic globalization. Around 50,000 people from all walks of life converged on Seattle to protest the third meeting of the World Trade Organization (WTO). The city was immobilized by people in the streets, and the meeting was disrupted. Among the demonstrators were children dressed as turtles, Korean priests playing drums and flutes, and thousands of labor union members. The Direct Action Network and other groups worked hard for months in advance training affinity groups in non-violent civil disobedience, and during the action communicated by cell phones to create blockades in the thirteen blocks around the downtown area, effectively isolating the WTO delegates in their hotels.

Jia Ching Chen, former Ruckus Society CD trainer commented, "It was amazing because you saw, even through the chaos, the crowd's spontaneity that helped shut down the conference. There were a lot of factors, including mistakes on the part of law-enforcement, that allowed this to happen. We trained for months and this allowed a huge mass direct action to join other segments of the protest. Without the action, labor activists wouldn't have been inspired to stay and support the more militant sections of the march."

Governmental Surveillance and Disruption:
COINTELPRO and Beyond

Every so often, community groups that really mobilize, educate, and organize effectively tend to catch the unfavorable attention of authorities. Imagine that one day you show up at your group's office a little early to get ready for a meeting. As you unlock the door, you notice that the office is a mess, with files and debris scattered all over the place. The computers don't seem to function well. Petty cash is still there as well as the tapes and the boombox.

This might seem farfetched, however, it is a scenario that many activists have faced over the years. It might be the price of effective organizing that someone will eventually try to scare you out of the game. The US Government has a very long rap sheet for crackdowns on activists, both non-violent and violent. In the 1910s the government deported thousands of immigrants who were suspected of being anarchist or socialist during the Palmer Raids. The black nationalist movement of Marcus Garvey was also infiltrated and investigated. These actions generated quite a bit of negative publicity, so the government learned to crackdown on dissent quietly.

COINTELPRO is the name that domestic covert action against social justice movements of the 1960s was known by. Ironically it was an act of direct action that exposed the program. In 1971 a group called the Citizens Committee to Investigate the FBI stole secret files from an FBI office and leaked them to the media.

Disruption can be broadly categorized by the following: 1) intelligence gathering, and 2) disruption and neutralization. The various tactics employed the government are meant to have multiple effects. For example, detectable surveillance (i.e., a van parked outside the office) may have the effect of gathering information but may be more intended for the effect of disruption by increasing paranoia and anxiety.Specifically, this can look like:

Inflaming Tensions Between Activists - Activists are opinionated people, and that is a good thing. However, our strong world views can be used against us, or be used to get us to turn against each other. Black liberation activists in the 1960s received anonymous notes accusing one another of interracial affairs, and other letters implying that certain activists were undercover agents. The rifts resulting from such tactics have split organizations and movements. Since activists aren't above the divided nature of the world, disrupters play upon racism, classism, sexism, and about any other -ism or division useful to them.

When accusations fly, it is important to stay calm and open-minded no matter how inflammatory they might be. This goes for sexual crimes, often some of the most hot button ones. Provide appropriate support for someone if they say they have been harmed; but never presume someone's guilt.

Also, never let political disagreements get personal. If you have serious disagreements with another activist over politics, make a special effort to build a respectful rapport with that person that is not based in trying to prove your point.

Protest the Protesters - Occasionally, activist groups are protested themselves usually around obscure charges. In one case, flyers accusing a movement leader of embezzlement were distributed to activists and government officials. Often the people who pull this kind of action off aren't agents (read: crazy wingnuts) but their actions are disruptive enough.

Break-Ins and Office Trashings - Organizational records are destroyed, suspicions aroused, people are scared to participate. In February 2002, the offices of the School of Unity and Liberation (SOUL) were broken into with many records and equipment lost. SOUL has been very active in anti-prison and anti-war organizing in the Bay Area.

The Taxman Cometh - Often, high-profile activists are subject to all sorts of curious audits and inquiries into their personal business.

Many forms of government disruption can be fought by following some common sense guidelines. The most common kind of disruption is not necessarily violent or flashy. Misinformation, most commonly about other activists is seeded, and people's half-baked reactions do the rest of the work. Remember, if someone is trying to stop you from your activism they are counting on you and your fellow activists to be susceptible to gossip, ideological bickering, sexism, racism and otherwise crappy ways of treating each other. These are organizational rifts that disrupters will take full advantage of in order to destroy a promising movement. Luckily, it doesn't take a counterintelligence expert to take the following precautions.

The following pointers are adapted from the highly recommended book *War At Home: Covert Action Against U.S. Activists and What We Can Do About It* by Brian Glick:

1. Check out the authenticity of any disturbing letter, rumor, phone call or other communication before acting on it. Ask the suspected source if he or she is responsible.

2. Keep record of any disturbing incident, and consider taking that information to the media. If you talk about such abuse in the media, avoid accusations against specific individuals or groups.

3. Always deal openly with issues of race, class, gender, sexuality, religion, and national origin. If people in your organization know that such differences can be dealt with respectfully, then your enemies cannot exploit these areas.

4. Don't ever expose anyone as an informer or disrupter without solid proof. Criticize suspicious actions, and expose the effect they have on the organization's work.

5. Support all movement activists that come under attack, even the ones you can't personally stand.

6. Get to know sympathetic journalists and build a network that can get the word out if your group becomes targeted for disruption.

7. While making certain that you don't accidentally spread misinformation yourself, don't tough out suspected disruption alone. High stress creates a breeding ground for bad judgement so make sure that you and your fellow activists get the rest and relaxation you need.

8. Most importantly, don't let them win. Keep organizing publicly. If you are ever targeted in a serious way, it will take support from a lot of people to pull through it.

9. Cultivate some reliable legal support that can help activists in jeopardy.

10. Keep multiple copies of important documents and databases far away from each other. After the September 11th attacks on New York's World Trade Center (WTC), the United States has entered into a bizarre chapter in the history of warfare and domestic civil liberties. On the one hand, the troops are out "defending liberty," while Congress has started to pass a whole mess of laws that dismantle exactly such liberties. Passed shortly after the tragedy, the USA PATRIOT act makes it easier for investigators to get wiretaps, intercept your e-mail, deport immigrants and curtail freedom of speech in regards to international causes not favored by the US Government. The act can also be seen as an attempt to roll back the modest reforms made following COINTELPRO's exposure.

John Viola, staff attorney with San Francisco's Coalition on Homelessness, observes, "Domestic intelligence activities continued in secrecy and with increasing sophistication until COINTELPRO was exposed in the mid-Seventies. Following the exposure of COINTELPRO, there was widespread demand for governmental reform of intelligence practices. Open government laws, the Freedom of Information Act, and prohibitions against interagency collaboration between the FBI and local law enforcement were products of this call for reform. Conservative political forces have never been happy with the limited controls placed on domestic intelligence and have long sought unfettered discretion for law enforcement to quell political dissent. The provisions in USA PATRIOT have little, if anything, to do with legitimate public safety concerns, but are very much about the repression of dissent."

The USA PATRIOT act may or may not have any longterm implications for civil disobedience activists, but knowing the history of COINTELPRO it is wise to take a few precautions that should be common sense anyhow. Many of the skills and attitudes needed to deal with increased police powers are the same needed to be a good activist.

- Don't discuss risky activities over the phone or on e-mail. Since authorities have the technical ability to monitor these transmissions, avoid giving them any extra information on your action.

- Know the risk levels of each participant before hand. If people in your group have special risk factors such as non-citizen or parole status, talk honestly about whether or not they should be on the front line for arrest. If the individual wants to do the action no matter what, and the group decides to allow it, then make plans in your legal support plan to deal with the situation.

Uniting and Strengthening America by Providing Appropriate Tools Required to Intercept and Obstruct Terrorism (USA PATRIOT ACT) Act of 2001 -

Title I: Enhancing Domestic Security Against Terrorism - Establishes in the Treasury the Counterterrorism Fund.

(Sec. 102) Expresses the sense of Congress that: (1) the civil rights and liberties of all Americans, including Arab Americans, must be protected, and that every effort must be taken to preserve their safety; (2) any acts of violence or discrimination against any Americans be condemned; and (3) the Nation is called upon to recognize the patriotism of fellow citizens from all ethnic, racial, and religious backgrounds.

(Sec. 103) Authorizes appropriations for the Federal Bureau of Investigation's (FBI) Technical Support Center.

(Sec. 104) Authorizes the Attorney General to request the Secretary of Defense to provide assistance in support of Department of Justice (DOJ) activities relating to the enforcement of Federal criminal code (code) provisions regarding the use of weapons of mass destruction during an emergency situation involving a weapon (currently, chemical weapon) of mass destruction.

(Sec. 105) Requires the Director of the U.S. Secret Service to take actions to develop a national network of electronic crime task forces throughout the United States to prevent, detect, and investigate various forms of electronic crimes, including potential terrorist attacks against critical infrastructure and financial payment systems.

(Sec. 106) Modifies provisions relating to presidential authority under the International Emergency Powers Act to: (1) authorize the President, when the United States is engaged in armed hostilities or has been attacked by a foreign country or foreign nationals, to confiscate any property subject to U.S. jurisdiction of a foreign person, organization, or country that he determines has planned, authorized, aided, or engaged in such hostilities or attacks (the rights to which shall vest in such agency or person as the President may designate); and (2) provide that, in any judicial review of a determination made under such provisions, if the determination was based on classified information such information may be submitted to the reviewing court ex parte and in camera.

Title II: Enhanced Surveillance Procedures - Amends the Federal criminal code to authorize the interception of wire, oral, and electronic communications for the production of evidence of: (1) specified chemical weapons or terrorism offenses; and (2) computer fraud and abuse.

(Sec. 203) Amends rule 6 of the Federal Rules of Criminal Procedure (FRCrP) to permit the sharing of grand jury information that involves foreign intelligence or counterintelligence with Federal law enforcement, intelligence, protective, immigration, national defense, or national security officials (such officials), subject to specified requirements.

Authorizes an investigative or law enforcement officer, or an attorney for the Government, who, by authorized means, has obtained knowledge of the contents of any wire, oral, or electronic communication or evidence derived therefrom to disclose such contents to such officials to the extent that such contents include foreign intelligence or counterintelligence.

Directs the Attorney General to establish procedures for the disclosure of information (pursuant to the code and the FRCrP) that identifies a United States person, as defined in the Foreign Intelligence Surveillance Act of 1978 (FISA).

Authorizes the disclosure of foreign intelligence or counterintelligence obtained as part of a criminal investigation to such officials.

(Sec. 204) Clarifies that nothing in code provisions regarding pen registers shall be deemed to affect the acquisition by the Government of specified foreign intelligence information, and that procedures under FISA shall be the exclusive means by which electronic surveillance and the interception of domestic wire and oral (current law) and electronic communications may be conducted.

(Sec. 205) Authorizes the Director of the FBI to expedite the employment of personnel as translators to support counter-terrorism investigations and operations without regard to applicable Federal personnel requirements. Requires: (1) the Director to establish such security requirements as necessary for such personnel; and (2) the Attorney General to report to the House and Senate Judiciary Committees regarding translators.

(Sec. 206) Grants roving surveillance authority under FISA after requiring a court order approving an electronic surveillance to direct any person to furnish necessary information, facilities, or technical assistance in circumstances where the Court finds that the actions of the surveillance target may have the effect of thwarting the identification of a specified person.

(Sec. 207) Increases the duration of FISA surveillance permitted for non-U.S. persons who are agents of a foreign power.

(Sec. 208) Increases (from seven to 11) the number of district court judges designated to hear applications for and grant orders approving electronic surveillance. Requires that no fewer than three reside within 20 miles of the District of Columbia.

(Sec. 209) Permits the seizure of voice-mail messages under a warrant.

(Sec. 210) Expands the scope of subpoenas for records of electronic communications to include the length and types of service utilized, temporarily assigned network addresses, and the means and source of payment (including any credit card or bank account number).

(Sec. 211) Amends the Communications Act of 1934 to permit specified disclosures to Government entities, except for records revealing cable subscriber selection of video programming from a cable operator.

(Sec. 212) Permits electronic communication and remote computing service providers to make emergency disclosures to a governmental entity of customer electronic communications to protect life and limb.

(Sec. 213) Authorizes Federal district courts to allow a delay of required notices of the execution of a warrant if immediate notice may have an adverse result and under other specified circumstances.

(Sec. 214) Prohibits use of a pen register or trap and trace devices in any investigation to protect against international terrorism or clandestine intelligence activities that is conducted solely on the basis of activities protected by the first amendment to the U.S. Constitution.

(Sec. 215) Authorizes the Director of the FBI (or designee) to apply for a court order requiring production of certain business records for foreign intelligence and international terrorism investigations. Requires the Attorney General to report to the House and Senate Intelligence and Judiciary Committees semi-annually.

(Sec. 216) Amends the code to: (1) require a trap and trace device to restrict recoding or decoding so as not to include the contents of a wire or electronic communication; (2) apply a court order for a pen register or trap and trace devices to any person or entity providing wire or electronic communication service in the United States whose assistance may facilitate execution of the order; (3) require specified records kept on any pen register or trap and trace device on a packet-switched data network of a provider of electronic communication service to the public; and (4) allow a trap and trace device to identify the source (but not the contents) of a wire or electronic communication.

(Sec. 217) Makes it lawful to intercept the wire or electronic communication of a computer trespasser in certain circumstances.

(Sec. 218) Amends FISA to require an application for an electronic surveillance order or search warrant to certify that a significant purpose (currently, the sole or main purpose) of the surveillance is to obtain foreign intelligence information.

(Sec. 219) Amends rule 41 of the FRCrP to permit Federal magistrate judges in any district in which terrorism-related activities may have occurred to issue search warrants for searches within or outside the district.

(Sec. 220) Provides for nationwide service of search warrants for electronic evidence.

(Sec. 221) Amends the Trade Sanctions Reform and Export Enhancement Act of 2000 to extend trade sanctions to the territory of Afghanistan controlled by the Taliban.

(Sec. 222) Specifies that: (1) nothing in this Act shall impose any additional technical obligation or requirement on a provider of a wire or electronic communication service or other person to furnish facilities or technical assistance; and (2) a provider of such service, and a landlord, custodian, or other person who furnishes such facilities or technical assistance, shall be reasonably compensated for such reasonable expenditures incurred in providing such facilities or assistance.

(Sec. 223) Amends the Federal criminal code to provide for administrative discipline of Federal officers or employees who violate prohibitions against unauthorized disclosures of information gathered under this Act. Provides for civil actions against the United States for damages by any person aggrieved by such violations.

(Sec. 224) Terminates this title on December 31, 2005, except with respect to any particular foreign intelligence investigation beginning before that date, or any particular offense or potential offense that began or occurred before it.

(Sec. 225) Amends the Foreign Intelligence Surveillance Act of 1978 to prohibit a cause of action in any court against a provider of a wire or electronic communication service, landlord, custodian, or any other person that furnishes any information, facilities, or technical assistance in accordance with a court order or request for emergency assistance under such Act (for example, with respect to a wiretap).

Title III: International Money Laundering Abatement and Anti-Terrorist Financing Act of 2001 - International Money Laundering Abatement and Financial Anti-Terrorism Act of 2001- Sunsets this Act after the first day of FY 2005 if Congress enacts a specified joint resolution to that effect.

Subtitle A: International Counter Money Laundering and Related Measures - Amends Federal law governing monetary transactions to prescribe procedural guidelines under which the Secretary of the Treasury (the Secretary) may require domestic financial institutions and agencies to take specified measures if the Secretary finds that reasonable grounds exist for concluding that jurisdictions, financial institutions, types of accounts, or transactions operating outside or within the United States, are of primary money laundering concern. Includes mandatory disclosure of specified information relating to certain correspondent accounts.

(Sec. 312) Mandates establishment of due diligence mechanisms to detect and report money laundering transactions through private banking accounts and correspondent accounts.

(Sec. 313) Prohibits U.S. correspondent accounts with foreign shell banks.

(Sec. 314) Instructs the Secretary to adopt regulations to encourage further cooperation among financial institutions, their regulatory authorities, and law enforcement authorities, with the specific purpose of encouraging regulatory authorities and law enforcement authorities to share with financial institutions information regarding individuals, entities, and organizations engaged in or reasonably suspected (based on credible evidence) of engaging in terrorist acts or money laundering activities. Authorizes such regulations to create procedures for cooperation and information sharing on matters specifically related to the finances of terrorist groups as well as their relationships with international narcotics traffickers.

Requires the Secretary to distribute annually to financial institutions a detailed analysis identifying patterns of suspicious activity and other investigative insights derived from suspicious activity reports and investigations by Federal, State, and local law enforcement agencies.

(Sec. 315) Amends Federal criminal law to include foreign corruption offenses as money laundering crimes.

(Sec. 316) Establishes the right of property owners to contest confiscation of property under law relating to confiscation of assets of suspected terrorists.

(Sec. 317) Establishes Federal jurisdiction over: (1) foreign money launderers (including their assets held in the United States); and (2) money that is laundered through a foreign bank.

(Sec. 319) Authorizes the forfeiture of money laundering funds from interbank accounts. Requires a covered financial institution, upon request of the appropriate Federal banking agency, to make available within 120 hours all pertinent information related to anti-money laundering compliance by the institution or its customer. Grants the Secretary summons and subpoena powers over foreign banks that maintain a correspondent bank in the United States. Requires a covered financial institution to terminate within ten business days any correspondent relationship with a foreign bank after receipt of written notice that the foreign bank has failed to comply with certain judicial proceedings. Sets forth civil penalties for failure to terminate such relationship.

(Sec. 321) Subjects to record and report requirements for monetary instrument transactions: (1) any credit union; and (2) any futures commission merchant, commodity trading advisor, and commodity pool operator registered, or required to register, under the Commodity Exchange Act.

(Sec. 323) Authorizes Federal application for restraining orders to preserve the availability of property subject to a foreign forfeiture or confiscation judgment.

(Sec. 325) Authorizes the Secretary to issue regulations to ensure that concentration accounts of financial institutions are not used to prevent association of the identity of an individual customer with the movement of funds of which the customer is the direct or beneficial owner.

(Sec. 326) Directs the Secretary to issue regulations prescribing minimum standards for financial institutions regarding customer identity in connection with the opening of accounts.

Requires the Secretary to report to Congress on: (1) the most timely and effective way to require foreign nationals to provide domestic financial institutions and agencies with appropriate and accurate information; (2) whether to require foreign nationals to obtain an identification number (similar to a Social Security or tax identification number) before opening an account with a domestic financial institution; and (3) a system for domestic financial institutions and agencies to review Government agency information to verify the identities of such foreign nationals.

(Sec. 327) Amends the Bank Holding Company Act of 1956 and the Federal Deposit Insurance Act to require consideration of the effectiveness of a company or companies in combating money laundering during reviews of proposed bank shares acquisitions or mergers.

(Sec. 328) Directs the Secretary take reasonable steps to encourage foreign governments to require the inclusion of the name of the originator in wire transfer instructions sent to the United States and other countries, with the information to remain with the transfer from its origination until the point of disbursement. Requires annual progress reports to specified congressional committees.

(Sec. 329) Prescribes criminal penalties for Federal officials or employees who seek or accept bribes in connection with administration of this title.

(Sec. 330) Urges U.S. negotiations for international cooperation in investigations of money laundering, financial crimes, and the finances of terrorist groups, including record sharing by foreign banks with U.S. law enforcement officials and domestic financial institution supervisors.

Subtitle B: Bank Secrecy Act Amendments and Related Improvements - Amends Federal law known as the Bank Secrecy Act to revise requirements for civil liability immunity for voluntary financial institution disclosure of suspicious activities. Authorizes the inclusion of suspicions of illegal activity in written employment references.

(Sec. 352) Authorizes the Secretary to exempt from minimum standards for anti-money laundering programs any financial institution not subject to certain regulations governing financial recordkeeping and reporting of currency and foreign transactions.

(Sec. 353) Establishes civil penalties for violations of geographic targeting orders and structuring transactions to evade certain recordkeeping requirements. Lengthens the effective period of geographic targeting orders from 60 to 180 days.

(Sec. 355) Amends the Federal Deposit Insurance Act to permit written employment references to contain suspicions of involvement in illegal activity.

(Sec. 356) Instructs the Secretary to: (1) promulgate regulations requiring registered securities brokers and dealers, futures commission merchants, commodity trading advisors, and commodity pool operators, to file reports of suspicious financial transactions; (2) report to Congress on the role of the Internal Revenue Service in the administration of the Bank Secrecy Act; and (3) share monetary instruments transactions records upon request of a U.S. intelligence agency for use in the conduct of intelligence or counterintelligence activities, including analysis, to protect against international terrorism.

(Sec. 358) Amends the Right to Financial Privacy Act to permit the transfer of financial records to other agencies or departments upon certification that the records are relevant to intelligence or counterintelligence activities related to international terrorism.

Amends the Fair Credit Reporting Act to require a consumer reporting agency to furnish all information in a consumer's file to a government agency upon certification that the records are relevant to intelligence or counterintelligence activities related to international terrorism.

(Sec. 359) Subjects to mandatory records and reports on monetary instruments transactions any licensed sender of money or any other person who engages as a business in the transmission of funds, including through an informal value transfer banking system or network (e.g., hawala) of people facilitating the transfer of money domestically or internationally outside of the conventional financial institutions system.

(Sec. 360) Authorizes the Secretary to instruct the United States Executive Director of each international financial institution to use his or her voice and vote to: (1) support the use of funds for a country (and its institutions) which contributes to U.S. efforts against international terrorism; and (2) require an auditing of disbursements to ensure that no funds are paid to persons who commit or support terrorism.

(Sec. 361) Makes the existing Financial Crimes Enforcement Network a bureau in the Department of the Treasury.

(Sec. 362) Directs the Secretary to establish a highly secure network in the Network that allows financial institutions to file certain reports and receive alerts and other information regarding suspicious activities warranting immediate and enhanced scrutiny.

(Sec. 363) Increases to $1 million the maximum civil penalties (currently $10,000) and criminal fines (currently $250,000) for money laundering. Sets a minimum civil penalty and criminal fine of double the amount of the illegal transaction.

(Sec. 364) Amends the Federal Reserve Act to provide for uniform protection authority for Federal Reserve facilities, including law enforcement officers authorized to carry firearms and make warrantless arrests.

(Sec. 365) Amends Federal law to require reports relating to coins and currency of more than $10,000 received in a nonfinancial trade or business.

(Sec. 366) Directs the Secretary to study and report to Congress on: (1) the possible expansion of the currency transaction reporting requirements exemption system; and (2) methods for improving financial institution utilization of the system as a way of reducing the submission of currency transaction reports that have little or no value for law enforcement purposes.

Subtitle C: Currency Crimes - Establishes as a bulk cash smuggling felony the knowing concealment and attempted transport (or transfer) across U.S. borders of currency and monetary instruments in excess of $10,000, with intent to evade specified currency reporting requirements.

(Sec. 372) Changes from discretionary to mandatory a court's authority to order, as part of a criminal sentence, forfeiture of all property involved in certain currency reporting offenses. Leaves a court discretion to order civil forfeitures in money laundering cases.

(Sec. 373) Amends the Federal criminal code to revise the prohibition of unlicensed (currently, illegal) money transmitting businesses.

(Sec. 374) Increases the criminal penalties for counterfeiting domestic and foreign currency and obligations.

(Sec. 376) Amends the Federal criminal code to extend the prohibition against the laundering of money instruments to specified proceeds of terrorism.

(Sec. 377) Grants the United States extraterritorial jurisdiction where: (1) an offense committed outside the United States involves an access device issued, owned, managed, or controlled by a financial institution, account issuer, credit card system member, or other entity within U.S. jurisdiction; and (2) the person committing the offense transports, delivers, conveys, transfers to or through, or otherwise stores, secrets, or holds within U.S. jurisdiction any article used to assist in the commission of the offense or the proceeds of such offense or property derived from it.

Title IV: Protecting the Border - Subtitle A: Protecting the Northern Border - Authorizes the Attorney General to waive certain Immigration and Naturalization Service (INS) personnel caps with respect to ensuring security needs on the Northern border.

(Sec. 402) Authorizes appropriations to: (1) triple the number of Border Patrol, Customs Service, and INS personnel (and support facilities) at points of entry and along the Northern border; and (2) INS and Customs for related border monitoring technology and equipment.

(Sec. 403) Amends the Immigration and Nationality Act to require the Attorney General and the Federal Bureau of Investigation (FBI) to provide the Department of State and INS with access to specified criminal history extracts in order to determine whether or not a visa or admissions applicant has a criminal history. Directs the FBI to provide periodic extract updates. Provides for confidentiality.

Directs the Attorney General and the Secretary of State to develop a technology standard to identify visa and admissions applicants, which shall be the basis for an electronic system of law enforcement and intelligence sharing system available to consular, law enforcement, intelligence, and Federal border inspection personnel.

(Sec. 404) Amends the Department of Justice Appropriations Act, 2001 to eliminate certain INS overtime restrictions.

(Sec. 405) Directs the Attorney General to report on the feasibility of enhancing the Integrated Automated Fingerprint Identification System and other identification systems to better identify foreign individuals in connection with U.S. or foreign criminal investigations before issuance of a visa to, or permitting such person's entry or exit from, the United States. Authorizes appropriations.

Subtitle B: Enhanced Immigration Provisions - Amends the Immigration and Nationality Act to broaden the scope of aliens ineligible for admission or deportable due to terrorist activities to include an alien who: (1) is a representative of a political, social, or similar group whose political endorsement of terrorist acts undermines U.S. antiterrorist efforts; (2) has used a position of prominence to endorse terrorist activity, or to persuade others to support such activity in a way that undermines U.S. antiterrorist efforts (or the child or spouse of such an alien under specified circumstances); or (3) has been associated with a terrorist organization and intends to engage in threatening activities while in the United States.

(Sec. 411) Includes within the definition of "terrorist activity" the use of any weapon or dangerous device.

Redefines "engage in terrorist activity" to mean, in an individual capacity or as a member of an organization, to: (1) commit or to incite to commit, under circumstances indicating an intention to cause death or serious bodily injury, a terrorist activity; (2) prepare or plan a terrorist activity; (3) gather information on potential targets for terrorist activity; (4) solicit funds or other things of value for a terrorist activity or a terrorist organization (with an exception for lack of knowledge); (5) solicit any individual to engage in prohibited conduct or for terrorist organization membership (with an exception for lack of knowledge); or (6) commit an act that the actor knows, or reasonably should know, affords material support, including a safe house, transportation, communications, funds, transfer of funds or other material financial benefit, false documentation or identification, weapons (including chemical, biological, or radiological weapons), explosives, or training for the commission of a terrorist activity; to any individual who the actor knows or reasonably should know has committed or plans to commit a terrorist activity; or to a terrorist organization (with an exception for lack of knowledge).

Defines "terrorist organization" as a group: (1) designated under the Immigration and Nationality Act or by the Secretary of State; or (2) a group of two or more individuals, whether related or not, which engages in terrorist-related activities.

Provides for the retroactive application of amendments under this Act. Stipulates that an alien shall not be considered inadmissible or deportable because of a relationship to an organization that was not designated as a terrorist organization prior to enactment of this Act. States that the amendments under this section shall apply to all aliens in exclusion or deportation proceedings on or after the date of enactment of this Act.

Directs the Secretary of State to notify specified congressional leaders seven days prior to designating an organization as a terrorist organization. Provides for organization redesignation or revocation.

(Sec. 412) Provides for mandatory detention until removal from the United States (regardless of any relief from removal) of an alien certified by the Attorney General as a suspected terrorist or threat to national security. Requires release of such alien after seven days if removal proceedings have not commenced, or the alien has not been charged with a criminal offense. Authorizes detention for additional periods of up to six months of an alien not likely to be deported in the reasonably foreseeable future only if release will threaten U.S. national security or the safety of the community or any person. Limits judicial review to habeas corpus proceedings in the U.S. Supreme Court, the U.S. Court of Appeals for the District of Columbia, or any district court with jurisdiction to entertain a habeas corpus petition. Restricts to the U.S. Court of Appeals for the District of Columbia the right of appeal of any final order by a circuit or district judge.

(Sec. 413) Authorizes the Secretary of State, on a reciprocal basis, to share criminal- and terrorist-related visa lookout information with foreign governments.

(Sec. 414) Declares the sense of Congress that the Attorney General should: (1) fully implement the integrated entry and exit data system for airports, seaports, and land border ports of entry with all deliberate speed; and (2) begin immediately establishing the Integrated Entry and Exit Data System Task Force. Authorizes appropriations.

Requires the Attorney General and the Secretary of State, in developing the integrated entry and exit data system, to focus on the use of biometric technology and the development of tamper-resistant documents readable at ports of entry.

(Sec. 415) Amends the Immigration and Naturalization Service Data Management Improvement Act of 2000 to include the Office of Homeland Security in the Integrated Entry and Exit Data System Task Force.

(Sec. 416) Directs the Attorney General to implement fully and expand the foreign student monitoring program to include other approved educational institutions like air flight, language training, or vocational schools.

(Sec. 417) Requires audits and reports on implementation of the mandate for machine readable passports.

(Sec. 418) Directs the Secretary of State to: (1) review how consular officers issue visas to determine if consular shopping is a problem; and (2) if it is a problem, take steps to address it, and report on them to Congress.

Subtitle C: Preservation of Immigration Benefits for Victims of Terrorism - Authorizes the Attorney General to provide permanent resident status through the special immigrant program to an alien (and spouse, child, or grandparent under specified circumstances) who was the beneficiary of a petition filed on or before September 11, 2001, to grant the alien permanent residence as an employer-sponsored immigrant or of an application for labor certification if the petition or application was rendered null because of the disability of the beneficiary or loss of employment due to physical damage to, or destruction of, the business of the petitioner or applicant as a direct result of the terrorist attacks on September 11, 2001 (September attacks), or because of the death of the petitioner or applicant as a direct result of such attacks.

(Sec. 422) States that an alien who was legally in a nonimmigrant status and was disabled as a direct result of the September attacks may remain in the United States until his or her normal status termination date or September 11, 2002. Includes in such extension the spouse or child of such an alien or of an alien who was killed in such attacks. Authorizes employment during such period.

Extends specified immigration-related deadlines and other filing requirements for an alien (and spouse and child) who was directly prevented from meeting such requirements as a result of the September attacks respecting: (1) nonimmigrant status and status revision; (2) diversity immigrants; (3) immigrant visas; (4) parolees; and (5) voluntary departure.

(Sec. 423) Waives, under specified circumstances, the requirement that an alien spouse (and child) of a U.S. citizen must have been married for at least two years prior to such citizen's death in order to maintain immediate relative status if such citizen died as a direct result of the September attacks. Provides for: (1) continued family-sponsored immigrant eligibility for the spouse, child, or unmarried son or daughter of a permanent resident who died as a direct result of such attacks; and (2) continued eligibility for adjustment of status for the spouse and child of an employment-based immigrant who died similarly.

(Sec. 424) Amends the Immigration and Nationality Act to extend the visa categorization of "child" for aliens with petitions filed on or before September 11, 2001, for aliens whose 21st birthday is in September 2001 (90 days), or after September 2001 (45 days).

(Sec. 425) Authorizes the Attorney General to provide temporary administrative relief to an alien who, as of September 10, 2001, was lawfully in the United States and was the spouse, parent, or child of an individual who died or was disabled as a direct result of the September attacks.

(Sec. 426) Directs the Attorney General to establish evidentiary guidelines for death, disability, and loss of employment or destruction of business in connection with the provisions of this subtitle.

(Sec. 427) Prohibits benefits to terrorists or their family members.

Title V: Removing Obstacles to Investigating Terrorism - Authorizes the Attorney General to pay rewards from available funds pursuant to public advertisements for assistance to DOJ to combat terrorism and defend the Nation against terrorist acts, in accordance with procedures and regulations established or issued by the Attorney General, subject to specified conditions, including a prohibition against any such reward of $250,000 or more from being made or offered without the personal approval of either the Attorney General or the President.

(Sec. 502) Amends the State Department Basic Authorities Act of 1956 to modify the Department of State rewards program to authorize rewards for information leading to: (1) the dismantling of a terrorist organization in whole or significant part; and (2) the identification or location of an individual who holds a key leadership position in a terrorist organization. Raises the limit on rewards if the Secretary State determines that a larger sum is necessary to combat terrorism or defend the Nation against terrorist acts.

(Sec. 503) Amends the DNA Analysis Backlog Elimination Act of 2000 to qualify a Federal terrorism offense for collection of DNA for identification.

(Sec. 504) Amends FISA to authorize consultation among Federal law enforcement officers regarding information acquired from an electronic surveillance or physical search in terrorism and related investigations or protective measures.

(Sec. 505) Allows the FBI to request telephone toll and transactional records, financial records, and consumer reports in any investigation to protect against international terrorism or clandestine intelligence activities only if the investigation is not conducted solely on the basis of activities protected by the first amendment to the U.S. Constitution.

(Sec. 506) Revises U.S. Secret Service jurisdiction with respect to fraud and related activity in connection with computers. Grants the FBI primary authority to investigate specified fraud and computer related activity for cases involving espionage, foreign counter-intelligence, information protected against unauthorized disclosure for reasons of national defense or foreign relations, or restricted data, except for offenses affecting Secret Service duties.

(Sec. 507) Amends the General Education Provisions Act and the National Education Statistics Act of 1994 to provide for disclosure of educational records to the Attorney General in a terrorism investigation or prosecution.

Title VI: Providing for Victims of Terrorism, Public Safety Officers, and Their Families - Subtitle A: Aid to Families of Public Safety Officers - Provides for expedited payments for: (1) public safety officers involved in the prevention, investigation, rescue, or recovery efforts related to a terrorist attack; and (2) heroic public safety officers. Increases Public Safety Officers Benefit Program payments.

Subtitle B: Amendments to the Victims of Crime Act of 1984 - Amends the Victims of Crime Act of 1984 to: (1) revise provisions regarding the allocation of funds for compensation and assistance, location of compensable crime, and the relationship of crime victim compensation to means-tested Federal benefit programs and to the September 11th victim compensation fund; and (2) establish an antiterrorism emergency reserve in the Victims of Crime Fund.

Title VII: Increased Information Sharing for Critical Infrastructure Protection - Amends the Omnibus Crime Control and Safe Streets Act of 1968 to extend Bureau of Justice Assistance regional information sharing system grants to systems that enhance the investigation and prosecution abilities of participating Federal, State, and local law enforcement agencies in addressing multi-jurisdictional terrorist conspiracies and activities. Authorizes appropriations.

Title VIII: Strengthening the Criminal Laws Against Terrorism - Amends the Federal criminal code to prohibit specific terrorist acts or otherwise destructive, disruptive, or violent acts against mass transportation vehicles, ferries, providers, employees, passengers, or operating systems.

(Sec. 802) Amends the Federal criminal code to: (1) revise the definition of "international terrorism" to include activities that appear to be intended to affect the conduct of government by mass destruction; and (2) define "domestic terrorism" as activities that occur primarily within U.S. jurisdiction, that involve criminal acts dangerous to human life, and that appear to be intended to intimidate or coerce a civilian population, to influence government policy by intimidation or coercion, or to affect government conduct by mass destruction, assassination, or kidnapping.

(Sec. 803) Prohibits harboring any person knowing or having reasonable grounds to believe that such person has committed or to be about to commit a terrorism offense.

(Sec. 804) Establishes Federal jurisdiction over crimes committed at U.S. facilities abroad.

(Sec. 805) Applies the prohibitions against providing material support for terrorism to offenses outside of the United States.

(Sec. 806) Subjects to civil forfeiture all assets, foreign or domestic, of terrorist organizations.

(Sec. 808) Expands: (1) the offenses over which the Attorney General shall have primary investigative jurisdiction under provisions governing acts of terrorism transcending national boundaries; and (2) the offenses included within the definition of the Federal crime of terrorism.

(Sec. 809) Provides that there shall be no statute of limitations for certain terrorism offenses if the commission of such an offense resulted in, or created a foreseeable risk of, death or serious bodily injury to another person.

(Sec. 810) Provides for alternative maximum penalties for specified terrorism crimes.

(Sec. 811) Makes: (1) the penalties for attempts and conspiracies the same as those for terrorism offenses; (2) the supervised release terms for offenses with terrorism predicates any term of years or life; and (3) specified terrorism crimes Racketeer Influenced and Corrupt Organizations statute predicates.

(Sec. 814) Revises prohibitions and penalties regarding fraud and related activity in connection with computers to include specified cyber-terrorism offenses.

(Sec. 816) Directs the Attorney General to establish regional computer forensic laboratories, and to support existing laboratories, to develop specified cyber-security capabilities.

(Sec. 817) Prescribes penalties for knowing possession in certain circumstances of biological agents, toxins, or delivery systems, especially by certain restricted persons.

Title IX: Improved Intelligence - Amends the National Security Act of 1947 to require the Director of Central Intelligence (DCI) to establish requirements and priorities for foreign intelligence collected under the Foreign Intelligence Surveillance Act of 1978 and to provide assistance to the Attorney General (AG) to ensure that information derived from electronic surveillance or physical searches is disseminated for efficient and effective foreign intelligence purposes. Requires the inclusion of international terrorist activities within the scope of foreign intelligence under such Act.

(Sec. 903) Expresses the sense of Congress that officers and employees of the intelligence community should establish and maintain intelligence relationships to acquire information on terrorists and terrorist organizations.

(Sec. 904) Authorizes deferral of the submission to Congress of certain reports on intelligence and intelligence-related matters until: (1) February 1, 2002; or (2) a date after February 1, 2002, if the official involved certifies that preparation and submission on February 1, 2002, will impede the work of officers or employees engaged in counterterrorism activities. Requires congressional notification of any such deferral.

(Sec. 905) Requires the AG or the head of any other Federal department or agency with law enforcement responsibilities to expeditiously disclose to the DCI any foreign intelligence acquired in the course of a criminal investigation.

(Sec. 906) Requires the AG, DCI, and Secretary of the Treasury to jointly report to Congress on the feasibility and desirability of reconfiguring the Foreign Asset Tracking Center and the Office of Foreign Assets Control to provide for the analysis and dissemination of foreign intelligence relating to the financial capabilities and resources of international terrorist organizations.

(Sec. 907) Requires the DCI to report to the appropriate congressional committees on the establishment and maintenance of the National Virtual Translation Center for timely and accurate translation of foreign intelligence for elements of the intelligence community.

(Sec. 908) Requires the AG to provide a program of training to Government officials regarding the identification and use of foreign intelligence.

Title X: Miscellaneous - Directs the Inspector General of the Department of Justice to designate one official to review allegations of abuse of civil rights, civil liberties, and racial and ethnic profiling by government employees and officials.

(Sec. 1002) Expresses the sense of Congress condemning acts of violence or discrimination against any American, including Sikh-Americans. Calls upon local and Federal law enforcement authorities to prosecute to the fullest extent of the law all those who commit crimes.

(Sec. 1004) Amends the Federal criminal code with respect to venue in money laundering cases to allow a prosecution for such an offense to be brought in: (1) any district in which the financial or monetary transaction is conducted; or (2) any district where a prosecution for the underlying specified unlawful activity could be brought, if the defendant participated in the transfer of the proceeds of the specified unlawful activity from that district to the district where the financial or monetary transaction is conducted.

States that: (1) a transfer of funds from one place to another, by wire or any other means, shall constitute a single, continuing transaction; and (2) any person who conducts any portion of the transaction may be charged in any district in which the transaction takes place.

Allows a prosecution for an attempt or conspiracy offense to be brought in the district where venue would lie for the completed offense, or in any other district where an act in furtherance of the attempt or conspiracy took place.

(Sec. 1005) First Responders Assistance Act - Directs the Attorney General to make grants to State and local governments to improve the ability of State and local law enforcement, fire department, and first responders to respond to and prevent acts of terrorism. Authorizes appropriations.

(Sec. 1006) Amends the Immigration and Nationality Act to make inadmissible into the United States any alien engaged in money laundering. Directs the Secretary of State to develop a money laundering watchlist which: (1) identifies individuals worldwide who are known or suspected of money laundering; and (2) is readily accessible to, and shall be checked by, a consular or other Federal official before the issuance of a visa or admission to the United States.

(Sec. 1007) Authorizes FY 2002 appropriations for regional antidrug training in Turkey by the Drug Enforcement Administration for police, as well as increased precursor chemical control efforts in South and Central Asia.

(Sec. 1008) Directs the Attorney General to conduct a feasibility study and report to Congress on the use of a biometric identifier scanning system with access to the FBI integrated automated fingerprint identification system at overseas consular posts and points of entry to the United States.

(Sec. 1009) Directs the FBI to study and report to Congress on the feasibility of providing to airlines access via computer to the names of passengers who are suspected of terrorist activity by Federal officials. Authorizes appropriations.

(Sec. 1010) Authorizes the use of Department of Defense funds to contract with local and State governments, during the period of Operation Enduring Freedom, for the performance of security functions at U.S. military installations.

(Sec. 1011) Crimes Against Charitable Americans Act of 2001 - Amends the Telemarketing and Consumer Fraud and Abuse Prevention Act to cover fraudulent charitable solicitations. Requires any person engaged in telemarketing for the solicitation of charitable contributions, donations, or gifts to disclose promptly and clearly the purpose of the telephone call.

(Sec. 1012) Amends the Federal transportation code to prohibit States from licensing any individual to operate a motor vehicle transporting hazardous material unless the Secretary of Transportation determines that such individual does not pose a security risk warranting denial of the license. Requires background checks of such license applicants by the Attorney General upon State request.

(Sec. 1013) Expresses the sense of the Senate on substantial new U.S. investment in bioterrorism preparedness and response.

(Sec. 1014) Directs the Office for State and Local Domestic Preparedness Support of the Office of Justice Programs to make grants to enhance State and local capability to prepare for and respond to terrorist acts. Authorizes appropriations for FY 2002 through 2007.

(Sec. 1015) Amends the Crime Identification Technology Act of 1998 to extend it through FY 2007 and provide for antiterrorism grants to States and localities. Authorizes appropriations.

(Sec. 1016) Critical Infrastructures Protection Act of 2001 - Declares it is U.S. policy: (1) that any physical or virtual disruption of the operation of the critical infrastructures of the United States be rare, brief, geographically limited in effect, manageable, and minimally detrimental to the economy, human and government services, and U.S. national security; (2) that actions necessary to achieve this policy be carried out in a public-private partnership involving corporate and non-governmental organizations; and (3) to have in place a comprehensive and effective program to ensure the continuity of essential Federal Government functions under all circumstances.

Establishes the National Infrastructure Simulation and Analysis Center to serve as a source of national competence to address critical infrastructure protection and continuity through support for activities related to counterterrorism, threat assessment, and risk mitigation.

Defines critical infrastructure as systems and assets, whether physical or virtual, so vital to the United States that their incapacity or destruction would have a debilitating impact on security, national economic security, national public health or safety, or any combination of those matters.

Authorizes appropriations.

Direct Action and Civil Disobedience

This chapter is written for those who are thinking about incorporating Civil Disobedience and Direct Action into protests, possibly for the first time. This is meant as an introduction, not the last word on the subject. Reactions from local authorities to these kinds of actions vary greatly.

Why Civil Disobedience and Direct Action?

Communities turn to the protest tactics of Civil Disobedience and Direct Action for a variety of reasons. When effective, CD/DA builds a sense of collective power that is much more profound then simply waiting for another election day to make a difference.

What's The Difference?

Generally speaking, CD is a tactic where the participants anticipate and often plan on getting arrested for the cause. Historically, participants use non-violent tactics and refuse to physically fight back, even when assaulted by police. DA is a tactic where there is an attempt to perform a disruptive action without arrest.

Obviously, most protest actions these days blur the distinctions between the two tactics, but it is important to go into an action knowing if your group intends to get arrested as part of a larger strategy. In either case, any kind of disruptive action can result in arrest, so be sure to plan accordingly.

A good example of the differences and similarities between the two approaches can be found in the San Francisco group, Homes Not Jails (HNJ), which uses both. Homes Not Jails is a ten-year-old activist organization that uses the Direct Action tactic of taking over vacant housing to protest homelessness. Every week, HNJ operates what is called an 'Away Team'. The team covertly identifies and opens up vacant housing and attempts to turn over that housing for the use of homeless people. These squats have sometimes lasted for months and stabilized homeless people's lives. This is a good example of the type of DA where the participants do not offer themselves up for arrest as a protest tactic. However, HNJ also uses public takeovers to provide a dramatic counter-spin to the overwhelmingly anti-homeless portrayal in the mass media. In San Francisco, the major daily newspapers stereotype homeless people as drug addicts and derelicts. Often HNJ takeovers have forced the media to portray an upbeat image of homeless people repairing dilapidated buildings that were community eyesores. This is an example of civil disobedience, since the participants are fully expecting that they will be arrested for their actions.

Planning

Some groups actually avoid any kind of planning when putting together an action, preferring to use spontaneity to decide whether or not to take risks. This is silly on a lot of levels. Planning increases your group's ability to get its point across and actually be spontaneous. Anytime an action could result in arrest, at least a few planning meetings are in order.

How should we dress? This might seem like a silly question but think about it — what is the image you are trying to project? The Civil Rights Movement protesters often wore their Sunday best to convey a sense of dignity and pride. The possibilities are endless. If you are all dressed up like turtles or in costume, what message will be conveyed? It is fun to strategize on such points of fashion with your group. Dress for success. Consider wearing business clothes, a suit if possible, and comfortable shoes. Comb your hair. This shows the media that it's not just 'anarchists' and 'radicals' that are demonstrating but a broad-based coalition from many backgrounds. Holding up a mirror to mainstream society can do a lot to further a cause and bring a message home.

When? If you are doing a sit-in, understand that arrests may not take place until the close of the work day, especially in government offices. If you want to minimize the time of your occupation, hit them near the end of the day. If you want to occupy the space for maximum media coverage, start earlier.

Earlier in the week is better than later. You never know what disaster might come around later in the week to knock your story right out of the docket. Don't bother planning an action on Fridays because Saturday papers are the least read of the week, unless it's centered on a specific event, e.g., the WTO meeting in Seattle.

Sundays are tricky as far as media is concerned. Some outlets have only a skeleton crew, but Sunday tends to be slow for news, so you may get more in-depth coverage. Also, Monday is the most read paper of the week so it might make sense to try an action Sunday.

Visual media: images speak louder than words. The best way to get your action on television is to make sure that you have strong visuals. Arrests are dramatic, but banners that clearly state your message are great as well. It is good to use a lot of color, but remember that black on white shows up better in a picture.

Experiment with banners and props that don't use words at all but get the message out with striking images. When you use words, use as few as possible.

Also remember that if you are going to be arrested, your message on a piece of clothing can be effective. The SF Print Collective has often made beautiful shirts for tenant activists with eye-catching slogans. As the activists were carted off to jail, their shirts spoke for them: 'Aqui Estamos y No Nos Vamos/We Are Here To Stay'.

Bring Identification, Not Contraband. Set clear ground rules for the people risking arrest. Don't bring anything you would have a problem with police discovering: drugs, weapons, or sensitive documents.

Affinity Groups

An affinity group is a small group of people gathered together to perform independent action within a larger demonstration. An affinity group can be as small as two people and increase in size from there. The advantages of affinity groups are: they allow for security, since you become familiar and have mutual support with your co-participants; increased flexibility for effective CDs; and an ability for groups to act according to conscience.

Watch out for those dynamic leaders - a single dynamic leader is easy to target, slander and marginalize. This is not good for that individual's health, or the morale and effectiveness of the movement. If you organize an affinity group it is important to go by certain ethical guidelines: don't take action that puts unsuspecting demonstrators at risk; and if your action is part of a coalition effort, devise clear lines of accountability. Affinity groups can also be used for actions not related to a mass demonstration, such as billboard "corrections," or other forms of covert direct actions.

An affinity group also allows you to devise roles for people who can't get arrested for whatever reason. Consider including the following roles in your group:

Arrestables. These are the people who put their bodies on the line in the action.

Traffic Control. If you are performing an action that is going to shut down car traffic, you should assign some of your most diplomatic comrades to soothe angry drivers' tempers.

Action Support. This could be anything such as providing food for people occupying a certain space, baby-sitting kids, moving arrestables' cars, or helping out with clean-up after a demonstration. The kind of action support offered could greatly affect who gets to participate in the action. Maybe the most revolutionary thing one could do is watching kids off-site and letting Mom take a turn at the front lines!

Media. When selecting a media spokesperson, think about who you are trying to reach down the line. If you want to send a message that people of color can speak for themselves, then make sure that people of color share the spokesperson's role.

Legal. Don't forget to have a legal observer, preferably but not necessarily a lawyer.

To Get A Permit?

Most cities in the United States require demonstrators to have a permit. When the demonstration is going to be a large gathering with speakers and music, it is generally a good idea to get one, since it gives an added level of legal protection. It can feel humiliating to ask the police for "permission" to protest. The best reason to get one is to responsibly deal with the fact that there will be people at your demonstration who have no interest whatsoever in getting arrested, and it is important to respect such individuals.

Use common sense about obtaining permits. If the demonstration is going to be small, or if absolute secrecy is required, then don't get a permit! Picketlines and press conferences do not need permits most of the time — unless you are using public space to hold your event. Avoid the permit process for acts of civil disobedience and direct action because an element of surprise often increases the action's effectiveness. A good example of this is the spectacular act of banner hanging. The tactic of banner hanging is a great method of attracting press attention and public awareness to a cause, and in most cases is a surefire recipe for an arrest. Generally banner hangers find a building strategically located so that the target of a campaign can see it and get the message. Members of the Ruckus Society scaled the main building of New York University to protest animal testing at the college. Had the Ruckus Society tipped off the police by asking for a permit for the protest, the building would have been closed off for hours. Instead a photograph of a gigantic banner with a picture of a tortured animal made it into the *New York Times*. A simple message that 'NYU's Labs are Making A Killing,' was broadcast to a very large audience.

Appoint Police Monitors and Police Liaisons

Your group should appoint Police Monitors and Police Liaisons (separate jobs). Police Monitors do what the name implies — keep an eye on the police, and record their actions and badge numbers. Often watching the police with videocameras can have a calming effect on the police. Who wants to be caught on tape opening up a can of ass-whooping on a protester? Use your best judgment with video since it can also be subpoenaed as evidence. Before the action, it may be very helpful to interview those risking arrest on-site in order to document their reasons for breaking the law. If they will be using a "Necessity Defense" in court (i.e. they had to commit this small crime in order to prevent a larger one), then establishing evidence of their intent will be valuable. Ask them who they are, what the date is, what they are doing here, how important are the issues to them, and what extreme conditions and frustrated attempts to work within the system (if any) have led them to this point in their campaign. Focus on what they perceive to be the larger issues involved. Try to put these interviews on a separate tape in case the whole tape is subpoenaed.

Every action and videotaping situation is different; be ready to move fast or to stay still, to let authorities know that they are being filmed or to stay hidden. Consider all your options. Take steps to ensure that you are able to stay on site and document what occurs. Dress appropriately. This might mean warm clothes, rain gear, layers or shorts and t-shirts. Or this may mean looking "mainstream and respectable," so as to attract as little attention to yourself as possible. In some situations you might want to obtain a press pass and present yourself as an "objective" journalist type. In other situations this might entail "setting up a blind" — a place where you can film the action area and remain hidden to authorities.

Get as close to the action or the subject as possible without getting caught or arrested or hurt. If you cannot get close, keep the subject/action framed as tightly and aesthetically as possible by filling the screen. Zooming in is often necessary, but increases the chances of shaking and an "artificial" look.

If the police are wrongfully arresting someone — or whenever you need to identify the police on hand — read off their badge numbers into the camera; this is faster than trying to zoom in and out on people that are moving.

Be mentally and physically prepared to remain non-violent in threatening situations and stick to the camera. Stay calm and focused. Having an assistant can be very helpful. They can run out hot footage, watch your back while you stare into your viewfinder, and look out for important shots that you might be missing.

Don't try to fulfill any other roles when you are the video witness support person or police monitor. Activists, organizers, and legal staff will be needing good video documentation of what occurs. Things may be getting crazy and violence may be happening, but the worse the situation gets, the more important it is for you to record the event on tape. If you will be the only person who can help people in danger, you did not plan your action well. You must remain taping to get that footage out of there and to the news, your legal help, even the cops if they were not involved. Be quiet and be attentive to getting good footage.

Police Liaisons are the only ones authorized to talk to the police and negotiate with them. Don't put any hot-tempered individuals in this role; and by all means make sure that the Liaison doesn't show up wearing a 'Fuck the Police' or 'Millions of Dead Cops' t-shirt! Conservative mainstream attire may make this job go a lot smoother. This is a major diplomacy role.

Jail Support

Jail support begins before the arrest. Either your lawyer or a volunteer will collect the names of the people placing themselves at risk. On this sheet there will also be a contact name of a friend or relative. It is important to have a grasp on how many people are in a risk situation.

After an arrest, providing that the police are playing by the book, the process goes in one of two ways. If the protester is being charged with a misdemeanor or an infraction, it is customary in some cities to simply 'cite out' non-violent protesters. In order for this to happen, a valid photo identification card is needed. Those with warrants out for other offenses or those who are not U.S. citizens should not risk arrest in an action. Parents getting arrested together should make sure their children are in the hands of good caretakers (preferably family), and that the caretaker has written permission to watch after the child.

If charged with a misdemeanor or an infraction, one must sign a citation. This citation is not an admission of guilt, but a promise to appear in court. If you do not appear in court or have an attorney appear for you, a bench warrant will be issued for your arrest.

If the protester is charged with a felony then a very different process begins. Police officers may charge protesters with felonies which they know will be dismissed by a judge — but the more serious charge allows them to detain the prisoner overnight. Be careful when planning a civil disobedience on a Friday, it is easy to spend the weekend in jail for relatively minor infractions.

Most civil disobedience charges are filed as misdemeanors and the protesters are cited out rather quickly, within 1-6 hours. Without becoming paranoid, it makes good sense to be prepared in case things go wrong. Research the specific booking procedures in your city, and assign roles for volunteers accordingly.

For example, if your city has an Own Recognizance (OR) program, as most do, then persons charged with non-violent felonies can be released without bail if they can convince the authorities that they are not a flight risk and will show up in court. Those providing jail support should have the name and phone number of the arrested's outside contact. They will then call that contact to let them know that he or she will be getting a call from an OR clerk or an agent of the court. That contact will have to be able to identify where the detainee works, where they live, and accurately say how long their friend has lived in the area. This information will have to match the information the detainee gives in their OR interview. OR witnesses should be wary of any questions asked that are beyond the scope of information needed to establish that she or he is not a flight risk.

If OR is denied then the protester has the right to see a judge the next day. Often the protester will find that most of the charges are dismissed, especially the most serious ones. If they are not, the protester can consult with a Public Defender or their own attorney as to the next course of action. The attorney can set a court date and negotiate for low or no bail.

You Have The Right To Remain Silent - Use It!

While in jail avoid talking about or joking about the action with fellow protesters or other inmates. Reading your Miranda Rights is a bit like conducting a Catholic Mass in Latin — hardly anyone does it anymore. Still you do have the right to not incriminate yourself. Police officers have different ways of interacting with protesters, some are insulting and others are quite friendly. In either case know that they are getting paid to collect evidence that can be used against you. Don't let an insulting cop provoke you into a rebuttal or an explanation of your actions. Don't let a friendly cop lull you into a conversation that you might regret later. Be aware that even a meaningless conversation about a football game could establish your whereabouts. Politely avoid unnecessary conversation. You only have to volunteer your name and current address.

HIV and Other Medical Considerations

The AIDS Coalition To Unleash Power (ACT-UP) is a DA/CD group which has probably made the most impact politically since the Civil Rights Movement. In the 1980s when AIDS first hit the United States, gay men were dying in the hundreds and thousands. Yet the Reagan administration wouldn't even admit that AIDS existed, much less devote and research to treatment or prevention. ACT-UP took to the streets challenging homophobic public officials and shutting down the New York Stock Exchange. ACT-UP had to contend with issues of HIV positive protesters disclosing their status when arrested. If you are HIV positive the decision to disclose is your own and no one can force you to do so. If police, or the jail nurse asks you to do so, try to avoid making such declarations unless you need access to medicines or treatment, which police are required to provide by law.

Voluntary and Informed Risk

The ethical protest organizer will make sure that everyone participating only assumes voluntary and informed risk of arrest and possible injury. Never put anyone into a situation where they could point to your organization as one that put them in danger against their will. This doesn't mean giving up the element of surprise, just be aware of points in the demonstration where it makes sense to let people know what your group will be attempting, and assisting them to safety if necessary.

The Race Question

After the 1999 Anti-World Trade Organization protests in Seattle, Elizabeth 'Betita' Martinez penned the widely circulated essay, "Where Was the Color in Seattle?" She wondered how actions protesting policies that mainly impacted communities of color managed to be largely white-dominated. This essay was a reality check to many activists in the growing anti-globalization movement. One could write volumes about how to overcome racism and exclusion in progressive direct action movements.

At the risk of oversimplifying, I would recommend considering the following points: Listen seriously to people from communities other than your own to understand how all kinds of protests are perceived. Understand that many people most affected by issues also have the most to lose in an arrest situation. Many people who may passionately agree with your group's stand on a issue might also have a completely different relationship with the police, the INS, child protective services, etc. You can get around this by collaborating with people to design actions and campaigns that have multiple ways to participate. Never let it seem like the ones who take on 'risky' actions are more important than those who don't.

John Sellers from the Ruckus Society agrees, "The movement is large if you consider the amount of people who are working on social justice issues. We always have to work to connect race, class, and gender with more solidarity; there are still a lot of barriers to break down internally."

Legal Issues

The National Lawyers Guild reminds us that whether or not you're a citizen, you have these basic constitutional rights:

The Right to Remain Silent. Although "Reading the Miranda," only happens in the movies these days, the Fifth Amendment still exists. You do not have to answer any questions beyond your name and address.

The Right to be Free from "Unreasonable Searches and Seizures". The Fourth Amendment is supposed to protect your privacy. This is a tricky area of law since we know that for many, this law is routinely violated. Keep note of any search activity the police performs on you while in custody. There is probably little you can do to prevent an illegal search; but it is possible to use this information in a court of law to prevent a conviction. When arrested, police generally have the right to search your body and property. However, if post-release an officer shows up at your house demanding to have a look around, they still need a search warrant.

The Right to Advocate for Change. The First Amendment to the U.S. Constitution protects the rights of groups and individuals who advocate changes in laws, government practices, and even the form of government. However, the INS can target non-citizens for deportation because of their First Amendment activities, as long as it could deport them for other reasons.

If the police officers are playing by the book, the arrest situation will go down something like the following. Often they do not play by the book. Mass protests bring out the worst in cops, they are nervous and angry and may not control their behavior in a professional manner.

One experienced civil disobedience participant arrested in the 1991 Gulf War protest at San Francisco's Federal Building passed on a suggestion from her mother's experience protesting the Vietnam War: "The cops may treat you better if they think you may be a lawyer, so wear a business suit. Also, getting arrested early in the day will often get you released early enough to allow you to lend support to other aspects of the action. When the local jails become full, the cops will often send arrestees to jails in other counties making further action that day impossible."

In the 1999 Seattle WTO demonstrations, police officers subjected protesters to tear gas, pepper spray, and riot batons. Be aware of that violence and police brutality may occur, and be in control of your own behavior. Decide in advance what your personal limits are.

Warning or Command

In many cities, it is the law that police officers must issue a warning or command before making an arrest. This isn't out of some kind of sense of fair play — it shields the police from lawsuits from onlookers swept up in the action. In the case of mass civil disobedience, police may not want to process hundreds of arrestees. Some cities are under a court-ordered consent decree to lessen jail overcrowding, and this can work to your advantage.

If the police say they will arrest in two minutes, allow anyone with second thoughts to leave without any misgivings or guilt trips. Make sure that an action support person can escort that person out of the area, since it is not unheard of for police to arrest people as they try to leave.

Arrest

Assume you are under arrest the minute a police officer touches you or seems to be impeding your ability to move freely through any means. You should make sure that everyone in your group has decided on a unified course of action BEFORE the arrest.

Decide in advance whether you are going to resist arrest or cooperate. Some civil disobedience activists advocate resisting at every step of the way. They use tactics such as "going limp," or otherwise making it hard to transport their body from arrest site to police van. If you take on this tactic, make sure that it matches the strategy of the group. Avoid any kind of macho posturing on this issue - people who resist arrest are no more "down for the cause" then people who don't. The decision to do so is purely tactical - are your group's aims served by a long arrest process or a short one? Keep in mind that *any* kind of resisting arrest can result in stiffer charges - even assault on an officer. Such charges don't normally hold up in court but can be used to extend jail time with a felony charge.

Don't panic. Visibly losing it isn't going to do you any good. To the contrary, it undermines the morale of your fellow arrestees. In most cases, you will be out of jail before long. Also, when authorities see prisoners of any type "going nuts" it often sends the signal that they might be able to lean on that individual for extra information that might incriminate themselves or others. Be as calm as a Buddha.

Processing and Booking

Do ask some basic questions. Politely ask whether or not you will be cited out or not, what your charges will be, and how long they expect to keep you. Don't expect an answer. If you believe you will be cited out, don't request a lawyer or three phone calls. In that case, being granted those things will extend your time in jail. Only demand these rights when it is obvious you are going to be kept there overnight or longer.

Don't fall for the good cop, bad cop routine. Sometimes a police officer playing the "bad cop" isolates an activist and tells him or her about how much trouble they are going to be in and how the book will be thrown at them, among other threats. Shortly thereafter, another officer will approach the activist and play the "good cop". They'll say things like "I know you're a good person, that's why you did what you did. My partner is having a real bad day, but if you tell me about how you pulled your action off, I'm sure we can get your charges dropped." Don't buy it! This is the oldest trick in the book, and unfortunately, one that a lot of people fall for. Anything you say can be used against you, so keep your mouth shut! Don't talk about the details of your action at all while in jail. It's one thing to tell other prisoners that there was a political action, and why people felt like it was necessary to risk arrest. Avoid telling anyone in jail anything else about the action. Someone facing a stiff sentence might be very easily manipulated into reporting to the police about anything you have told them.

Decide in advance whether or not you are using jail solidarity. Jail solidarity is a tactic where each individual arrested in an action refuses to be released until everyone is. This can be an effective tactic when placed in an overcrowded jail under court order to reduce the prisoner load. Many times this is unnecessary – under most circumstances protesters are cited out one by one. Once released, a protester can take on responsibilities such as calling friends and family of those still in jail, or talking to the media. Generally, jail solidarity is a necessary tactic if one member of the arrested is being targeted for any reason or being denied access to necessary medicine.

There is a good chance that you won't even make it this far and will be cited out quickly.

First Date In Court

Usually, your first day in court is simply when charges are either dropped or amended, and future court dates are set. If you will be using a Public Defender, then you will meet him or her then as well. If you get a PD, have an honest discussion about what kind of deals they think are appropriate to cut in your case, and whether or not they feel they can represent you with full enthusiasm and professionalism. Most PDs are overworked and may view your case cynically, since they are representing many dozens of people who did not have the luxury of "choosing" to be arrested. You always have the right to ask for new counsel.

If you haven't made a court strategy from the beginning, then be sure to make one with your fellow arrestees before your court date. Things to consider: What will happen if you are offered a deal? Can all members of your group afford to go to a drawn out trial?

There is also the matter of political strategy. Some groups will reject any plea bargains, in order to "put the system on trial." This should be done in consultation with an attorney in order to weigh the potential gains and risks. Remember, judges tend to be well connected with the political elite that you made trouble for in the first place. Don't be so naive as to think you will get a fair trial! If you do decide, or are forced to a trial, insist on a jury.

The Trial

A trial is another potential opportunity to gain support for the cause that landed you in jail in the first place. If you have to go to trial make sure that your group forms a media strategy to support both your case and the larger issue. Packing the courtroom with supporters at this point is recommended.

Verdict and Sentencing

If a guilty verdict is rendered, letters from community members for lenient sentencing can have some effect, especially if the judge has to run for election. Packing the courtroom with supporters at this point too is essential. Most non-violent civil disobedience verdicts are fairly light, and involve little or no jail time. Often, the sentence may be many hours of community service and probation. In the case of a longer sentence, the group and community should have thought out ways to support the prisoner while they are away. For example, if an activist is sentenced to six months in prison, how will their community make sure their rent is paid for, animals taken care of, medical needs supported, messages relayed, etc.? Benefits can be held, and funds can be raised, as well as awareness of the case through the media.

Federal Government/Property

Generally, if an action is committed inside or on federal property, the federal marshals have jurisdiction. However, most cities have mutual aid agreements with the feds, so it is conceivable that local police could be called in. Nevertheless the processing of the arrest is likely to be done by the feds.

If the action happens outside of the federal property, then either body could handle the arrest and processing. A good example of this is the standard blockade of the building. The sidewalk is within the jurisdiction of the local police, but the building and part of the surrounding area (such as plazas and walkways) are federal. This means that in any protest around federal property arrested people could be split up and taken to local jails and federal jails. A legal strategy should take this into account and know the procedures for both.

Most places have "concurrent jurisdiction" rules meaning that both local and federal police can arrest protesters.

Kim Malcheski, people's attorney extraordinaire, a man responsible for many activists' continued freedom, compiled this list of ten things you should know before you are arrested:

1. If you want to get out of jail ASAP, you should carry a current picture ID card. If you do not have a valid ID, the police do not have to cite you; i.e. have you sign a citation or promise to appear. By signing a citation, you only agree to appear in court on a certain day.

2. If you give the police a false or fake name, you could be charged with another misdemeanor. If you refuse to give a name, you could be charged with resisting or interfering with a police officer.

3. If you are arrested and booked into jail in California (and many other states) on state charges, you have a right to make three phone calls to a lawyer, bail bondsman, and family member.

4. If you are arrested, the police do not have to read you your Miranda rights ("you have the right to remain silent,....."). The police only have to read you your Miranda rights when you are actually questioned by police in custody.

5. You only have to tell the police your name, address, and date of birth. You do not have to reveal your immigration status. Do not volunteer any other information to the police or make any statements. If they question you, tell them you want to speak to a lawyer. Do not answer any other questions.

6. If you physically resist a cop who is trying to arrest you, they will probably beat you up and charge you with resisting arrest and battery. You should never touch a cop.

7. If you are arrested, the police can search your person and your possessions, so you should not carry any contraband, weapons, illegal drugs, etc. Do not bring any politically sensitive papers to protests.

8. Even if you are arrested on certain charges, the district attorney (who files formal criminal charges in court) can drop the charges, or file new or different charges. If you are charged with a misdemeanor or felony in state court, you have the right to a court-appointed lawyer if you cannot afford one.

9. If you are on parole or probation, you should think twice about risking arrest because your probation or parole can be revoked without a jury trial, and you could be sent to jail or prison.

10. If you are ever served with a subpoena to testify before a grand jury or in court, you should immediately speak to an attorney. You may have legal grounds (i.e. the Fifth and First Amendments) to refuse to testify. Never appear before a grand jury without a lawyer to advise you.

Civil disobedience is tricky because it makes an appeal for those in power to use their power in a responsible way. If such power wasn't being abused, then political action in general would be a lot less necessary. Many of us know from experience that no list of rights will guarantee the gracious behavior of an arresting officer. These guidelines are meant to minimize risks and provide activists with a beginning for establishing effective plans. Never assume that you'll get off easy because your cause is just. Stay flexible but prepared.

Raising a Ruckus

The Ruckus Society is a sort of school for protesters to learn non-violent civil disobedience. The group never fails to live up to its name, playing pivotal roles in the anti-globalization movement, and a growing number of local and environmental struggles.

Ruckus situates itself in a long tradition of non-violent social change. Founded in 1995, hundreds of activists have attended their Action Camps where the safe and effective use of disruption is taught. The organization places much emphasis on 'breaking the mass-media blockade,' and often designs actions with the evening news in mind.

The society is most famous for its role in large-scale disruptions of events such as the World Trade Organization protests and the Republican National Convention 2000. They are committed to the type of non-violent tactics that do not seem at all passive or wimpy. The Ruckus signature actions are the hanging of large banners on tall buildings, urban lockdowns that tie up traffic all day, and environmental defense. The group has been so effective that police have started to arrest leaders before they actually commit a crime. During the Republican Convention, executive director John Sellers was arrested under the suspicion of using a cell phone to direct a protest.

John Sellers first started using civil disobedience and direct action while working for Greenpeace in 1990. The first time he observed direct action was when he witnessed a band of "little old ladies" shut down a missile site. Both of his parents were active in labor unions – his mother was a teacher and his father was a member of the United Rubber Workers Union. He recalls walking picket lines with his parents every few years. His aunts were activists and took him to the "No Nukes" rally in New York as a kid.

His advice for people on participating in their first civil disobedience arrest? "You have to breathe, stay calm and hold on to your humanity. The system is structured to rob you of your humanity, so you have to project yours forward. Be quiet within yourself and be respectful. I've seen activists give each other high-fives in the holding cell, which can be disrespectful of the people who are in there, punished for poverty or racism. Listen and learn and be observant. Get to know your new environment before you interact with it."

The most important thing that the Ruckus Society does is train new civil disobedience activists in how to be effective and safe. The second most important thing they do is to seize the media, who often hate to give activists media airtime. Ruckus thrives in the world of simple and clear messages: picture a gigantic banner hanging off a tall construction crane. Painted on the banner is an arrow with the word Democracy imbedded in it. Pointing the opposite direction is another arrow that says WTO. That picture was seen all around the world, providing a little political context in a time when the media would have rather have focused on sensationalism instead of issues.

The Ruckus Society is unique in that it carries on no specicfic campaigns or causes of its own. It teaches activists how to safely and effectively incorporate direct action and civil disobedience into their work. Ruckus began as a support for environmental efforts; now its signature can be seen at protests for economic, racial and animal rights. The group is most known for its involvement with the disruption of the Democratic and Republican Conventions 2000, D.C. Protest of the International Monetary Fund, and the infamous Seattle Protest of the WTO.

The Houston Chronicle wrote about Ruckus, "These are the people who chain themselves to giant logging machines, form human chains in front of nuclear waste dump sites, rappel from the roofs of skyscrapers or dangle hundreds of feet off bridges - all to bring attention to the environmental, ecological or social justice cause du jour... They are college dropouts and campus hangers-on, holders of graduate degrees, moms, grandmothers, married women, single mothers, lesbians and even some former mid-level management types."

"We have a lot of people come here skeptical, that it's a boot camp or a hippie woo-woo camp. And we're neither," said co-founder Mike Roselle, whose activist roots include the in-your-face environmental groups Greenpeace and Earth First!. "We basically teach old-fashioned, all-American civil disobedience."

During the Republican National Convention in 2000, local police were certainly aware of Ruckus's effectiveness, and launched a series of preemptive strikes to shut down the protests. Ruckus co-founder and executive director John Sellers was arrested for possession of an "instrument of a crime," in his case a cell phone. Police used every trick at their disposal to keep Sellers off the streets during the convention, including refusing to accept bail money and refusal to process his release until a Social Security number was furnished.

Sellers was originally given one million dollars bail—unheard of since he was only charged with a series of misdemeanors. Other would-be protesters were given bails as high as $500,000. It was widely speculated that such preemptive actions were designed to take out key leaders and weaken the protests. Since the actions were structured around decentralized leadership, the absence of one important player did not hamper the movement. Assistant District Attorney Cindy Martelli asserted that Sellers "facilitates the more radical elements to accomplish their objective of violence and mayhem," although the Philadelphia protests were remarkably free of much protester-initiated violence or property damage.

The Ruckus Society outlines five reasons for a civil disobedience or direct action:

ANNOUNCEMENT OR ALARM This type of action exposes the 'hidden hands' behind an injustice or breaks the media silence around an ongoing issue.

REINFORCEMENT Often, an activist group can do all the letter writing campaigns, petition drives, meetings with powerful people—and end up with nothing. The general public doesn't even have an opinion on the issue since so little debate has been generated. This type of action strives to convey the issue in simple terms to a larger audience.

PUNCTUATION An organizing campaign naturally has high and low profile parts. It's good to keep an issue alive through action, especially if the campaign is waiting upon decisions from policy makers or politicians. This drives home the point that the real power is in the community—not the back rooms.

ESCALATION Most community organizing schools of thought teach activists to escalate confrontation strategically, expending 'within the system' options in order to build public support for confrontation. When interests are entrenched, it is a rule of thumb that they won't yield to demands quickly or without a fight. Escalation is also most effective when it is combined with a form of economic disruption. Most movements do not make noticeable headway until they start costing someone money.

MORALE Collective, confrontational action builds alliances as well as group and self discovery. Careful with using such actions solely for morale purposes—that can backfire especially if there will be legal entanglements afterwards.

Checklist for Effective Direct Action Media
from The Ruckus Society Media Manual

One month to one week before the action

Decide what person or persons will be in charge of media strategy. The benefits of consensus aside, it is nearly impossible to write a press release, focus on a key sound bite, contact key reporters, or accomplish any other media tasks by committee. So empower a media team to make these decisions, and let them do their jobs without second-guessing and micro-managing.

The most logical makeup of the media team is a media coordinator, an action coordinator and the lead campaigner. During the action itself, each of these people will likely be stationed at a point where they can serve as media spokespersons. If the media coordinator is to be stationed at the action site, you need one more member of the team: Someone to stay in an office and work the fax machine (unless you have on-site fax capability).

Settle on one simple message. Accept it: You're not going to be able to communicate all the points, sub-points and shades of gray about the issue you'd like to. An action is like a freeway billboard, designed to hammer home one — and almost always only one — message. If you can't focus on one issue that's the main reason you're doing the action, you shouldn't be doing the action at all.

Choose a strong image that clearly communicates the message. Remember the freeway billboard: With one glance it is (or should be) unmistakable what product or idea is being sold. Ideally, your action should communicate the message without any words of explanation — and always in as few as possible.

If you find yourself saying, "They'll understand it when they read the banner," your image isn't clear enough. But the banner, which will probably contain language very similar to the sound bite, must also be capable of communicating the message on its own. You may not pull off the image; or you may not get the banner up; each, therefore, has to be able to stand alone.

Craft sound bites that communicate the message and enhance the image. Assemble the media team. Take out a legal pad. Lock the door. Throw out short, simple, declarative sentences that express your message. (Remember: The average sound bite on U.S. tv is less than ten seconds.) Write them down. Stay in the room until you have five that might work. From five, choose three. From three, choose one. Shape and refine it until it's as close to perfect as hard work and creativity can make it.

Choose a date and hour for the action that will maximize your chances for coverage. Sometimes you have to do an action when it is possible to do it, or when it's safe to do it. But if circumstances permit you to choose the date and time, make your choices with the media's convenience in mind. Again, there's no formula, but there are some general rules of thumb:

- Morning is better than afternoon. Almost no event short of a major catastrophe gets covered on the evening news, or in the next morning's paper, if it occurs after 3 p.m.

- Monday through Thursday are the best days, and Monday's best of all, because the later you go in the week, the greater the chance that some other big story will come along and blow you off the news map. Avoid Friday (lowest tv viewership Friday night; lowest newspaper readership Saturday morning; lots of competing news). Saturday and Sunday are also not the best, because news outlets operate with skeleton crews on weekends.

- Combining the above guidelines, we arrive at the theoretical best time for a hypothetical action: 10:30 a.m. on Monday, after news crews have reported to work for the day, but before they've got other stories going. But that's assuming your action occurs in a news vacuum, which it won't. Try to time the action so that it either anticipates or responds to an event the media will recognize as a story — "the news peg." If the President plans to sign the bill you're protesting on Thursday, do your action on Wednesday.

One week to a few days before the action
Write a draft press release. Circulate the draft release to the media team. Discuss and revise, discuss and revise, until it's perfect or you need to move on. Remember: The press release is not the message. It also is not the action. The action is the message. The press release is an advertisement to get the media to cover your action. The first two paragraphs are far more important than the rest of the release; the headline is even more important than that.

Make a list, with phone and fax numbers, of every news outlet you can think of that might be interested in the story.

If you have time before the action, consult a media directory. The standard national references are the Bacon's News Media Guides, with geographically indexed volumes for print and broadcast. (Bacon's, 332 S. Michigan Ave., Chicago, IL 60604.) They're expensive, but available in good libraries. Or try to find a directory for your state or region, which may be published by a press club or the like. In a pinch, get out your Yellow Pages.

Check the phone number and fax number listed in the directory to make sure they're correct. Prioritize this list in order of most important outlets, but remember: The Associated Press is (almost) always first.

Begin practicing sound bites and mock interviews with the media team. If someone's never been interviewed on camera and you have one available, videotape each other, play it back and look carefully for anything — words, gestures, expressions, mannerisms, posture — that doesn't enhance effective communication. Practice until you eliminate those things. Decide what supplementary materials (fact sheets, background papers, maps, etc.) are needed for the press kit. Assemble the materials and folders to put them in. Get them all ready to go, except for the press release, which you'll add after any last-minute changes

A few days to one day before the action
Gut check: Decide if it's safe to tip off key reporters in advance. If there are one or two reporters whose coverage is key, and you

decide they can be trusted, approach them now — strictly off the record — and let them know what's going to happen. You may find out they'll be out of town, but they can tell you who will be covering in their place. They may tell you they live two hours away, so they need extra notice. They may want to cover the action from a strategic vantage point. Make adjustments to accommodate them if you can, but never at the expense of a safe, effective, authentic action.

The day before the action

Finalize the press release. If at all possible, keep it to one page. Spell-check it. Proofread it. Get someone else to proofread it again. Print it, copy it and add it to the press kits.

Alert all media you can trust, and who might possibly want to be on the scene, that the action is going down.

Obviously, there are times when you can't tell anyone. The local newspaper may be in the pocket of the industry you're hitting. The tv anchor in a small market may not know enough not to "accidentally" break a pledge of confidentiality. But in general, if you approach the news media straightforwardly and make sure that you're off the record, they will honor your request to keep the information confidential.

Sometimes you just have to take a deep breath and take a chance, because if news outlets know what's coming you're almost certain to get better coverage. But do not, under any circumstance, fax them the press release, or anything else except a map — nothing on paper until the action is safely under way. Faxes can be lost or intercepted.

Ideally, you should speak directly with the reporter who's going to cover the story. If that's not possible, you should ask to speak to the city editor of a newspaper, and the assignment editor of a tv or radio station. Be prepared to tell them in 30 to 60 seconds what you're doing, why you're doing it and why it will make a good story. Make sure they get the exact time and place of the action, and phone numbers where you or someone else on the media team can be reached from that moment until the action.

The best time to do this round of calls is the late morning or early afternoon before the action. Before 11 a.m., most editors are in meetings; after 4 p.m. they are on deadline and they will not want to talk to you. If you can't call before 4 wait until 7 p.m. and call the night editor.

If you know you'll have reporters on the scene when the action starts — or even think you might have some — do whatever you can to keep news cameras away from the actual site until the action is underway. Have them meet you at a nearby staging area and take them in once your activists are in place. Or tell them to be there half an hour after you expect things to be in place, if you can control the timing that closely.

The night before the action

At a meeting of everyone involved (action people, ground protesters, support people) go over the press release, emphasizing the main message and the lead sound bite.

Spend some time with everyone who might possibly be in an arrest or interview situation, letting them practice the sound bite or variations on it. If there are too many of you, partner off and practice in pairs.

The morning of the action

Get on the phone by 7:30 a.m. (assuming it's a morning action, which is almost always best for coverage).

Call the tv and radio stations again, to make sure someone on the news desk got the message from the day before and knows what's happening. Again make sure they have the exact time, place and the correct phone numbers for contacts. Most newspapers won't have someone on the desk until 9 a.m.; call them if time permits.

Double check to make sure that the person stationed at the fax machine has copies of the release and the prioritized list of news outlets.

As soon as the action begins

You "have an action" at the moment protesters are in place and/or the image and banner are deployed. If you are some distance from the action site, work out a radio signal with the action coordinator, who should notify you the instant this occurs. Then: Contact the person at the fax machine and tell them to start pumping out the faxes. It is ideal, if you have the capability, to use multiple fax machines or to pre-store the list of numbers in your fax machine so you can start the process with one command. Do your best, but anything that gets out the maximum number of faxes in the shortest amount of time will help.

Begin calling, in order of priority, the news outlets on your fax list. Identify yourself by name and organization, and clearly and succinctly, inform that you have a peaceful protest underway, its location and the purpose. Be calm and businesslike, not urgent or lecturing.

For example: "This is Zazu Pitts with Rainforest Action Network. This morning we are conducting a peaceful, nonviolent protest against Unocal's destruction of the Amazon. Five minutes ago, two climbers scaled to the top of Unocal's headquarters in downtown Los Angeles, and they're going to stay there until the company agrees to meet with us."

At that point, they'll usually say: "Send us a press release." Tell them one is on its way, then say something like: "I just wanted to tell you the protest is going on right now at 123 Main Street, let you know how to reach us, and see if I can answer any questions for you." They'll either say no thanks, or start asking questions. For an action in a major U.S. metropolitan area, these will almost surely be the first few calls you make: the Associated Press; United Press International and/or Reuters; the 3 or 4 leading TV news stations; the 2 or 3 leading radio news stations; the local newspaper.

If you're in a smaller town — one without an AP bureau or tv station — your first calls may be the local newspaper and radio station. But get in touch with the closest AP office as soon as possible.

During the action

Do not keep calling back with updates, unless they are truly big and unexpected developments. If the outlets are interested, they will be following the action through the authorities.

With cellular telephones, it is now common for action protesters to speak live to the news media from where they are hanging or locked down. News radio stations in particular love this, so if you didn't reach them at the beginning of the action, keep trying and make sure they know they can go live to the site.

It's best to let the people who are actually engaged in direct action deliver the message, it adds undeniable authenticity to the coverage. As media coordinator you should of course also be prepared to deliver crisp, on-message sound bites. But your main responsibility is to help journalists do their jobs.

Reporters will ask all kinds of questions unrelated to the action's message, e.g. How do they go to the bathroom up there? You should be ready to provide a courteous answer that nonetheless quickly turns back to the topic at hand. ("They wear diapers. It's inconvenient, but that's nothing compared to the danger this toxic waste poses to this community.")

After the action

When the protesters are arrested, or leave peacefully, or whatever marks the end of the action, call the main outlets mentioned above (at least, those that showed any interest at all) and tell them that the protest ended, what time it ended, and the outcome. Again, make sure they know where you can be reached the rest of the day, and often the following day. If there were arrests and people are released later that day, call again with that update.

For extensive updated media info, go to www.ruckus.org

Poem for an Activist Who Doubts Herself
by Dani Montgomery

We're standing on the curb smoking
and you raise your face to the sky
wanting to know why couldn't i have been around back
in the seventies?
you read books about struggle and feel small.
you walk along fillmore in the february wind
while cops circle the block again and again
wondering how come
in a time when so many grow up
and go out
without even the hope
of enough
why when we need a movement
more than ever

there's less and less talk of revolution?

and like you said
we need more than a job center
a drop in clinic
more than a free meal
more than a few lives saved.
we need more than this block
more than this city
more than five hundred
or five thousand marching.

but we're two
and upstairs in the office there's three more
cutting flyers and making phone calls
and at the senior center down the street
we could find six and seven
been sitting alone in their rooms
without enough cash for taxi fare
and on the bus
i know we could get eight, nine, ten
out of work
riding up and down town all day
filling out forms in the hope of a bed tonight and
there's number eleven
counting out rolls of pennies in safeway

yesterday in juvie i met twelve through twenty
armed with pencils
and they have mothers and lovers and brothers and
friends
who have a niece and a godson and a downstairs
neighbor
and we'll get to enough.
We'll be the light on our granddaughters' faces
when they pierce the sky with victory.

Resources

Civil Disobedience and Protest Tips

Act-Up New York has the finest on-line CD manual I know of. It is constantly being revised and improved. You'll see why this group was so effective taking on Ronald Reagan's 'see-no-virus' approach to the early epidemic. http://www.actupny.org

Housing Action is a growing but loose network of groups and activists that combine civil disobedience, legislative work, guerilla lobbying and community organizing to affect housing issues on a national scale. Contact the National Coalition on Homelessness (202)737-6444 x12   housingaction@yahoogroups.com

The Ruckus Society gives a lot of technical support to groups wishing to use CD. Not only is the website useful, but it captures a lot of the excitement around such protests. The website has an excellent primer on the media. 4131 Shafter Avenue, Suite 9 Oakland, CA 94609 (510)595-3442 (510)595-3462 ruckus@ruckus.org   http://www.ruckus.org/

Legal Support

Center For Constitutional Rights, 666 Broadway, New York, NY 10012, (212) 614-6464, www.ccr-ny.org

National Lawyers Guild is an organization of lawyers who have been watching out for your right to dissent for a long time now. Most of their documents are on-line. They also provide top-notch legal observation for demonstrations and Know Your Rights trainings for everyone. 126 University Place, Fifth Floor, New York, NY 10003, (212)627-2656, www.nlg.org

Making The Media Work For The People

Media Alliance - 814 Mission Street, #205, San Francisco, CA 94103 (415) 546-6334; classes (415) 546-6 491;fax (415) 546-6218 info@media-alliance.org
East Coast: 450 West 33rd Street, New York, New York 10001; (212)560-2919; mediaall@thirteen.org

Whispered Media - PO Box 40130 San Francisco, CA 94142 wm@videoactivism.org

Indymedia is a collective of independent media organizations and hundreds of journalists offering grassroots, non-corporate coverage. http://www.indymedia.org.

Art

An excellent source of hands-on information on how to make puppets and props for actions is The Puppeteers' Cooperative. They offer a manual for $4 and a video for $10. The Puppeteers' Cooperative - http://www.gis.net/~puppetco/index.html email: 0002136581@mcimail.com

Books for Further Reading

Branch, Taylor *Pillar of Fire, America in the King Years 1963-65* 1998 (Touchstone)

Glick, Brian *War At Home: Covert Action Against US Activists and What We Can Do About It* 1989 (South End Press)

Lynd, Staughton, ed., *We Are All Leaders, The Alternative Unionism of the Early 1930s* 1996 (University of Chicago Press)

Yuen, Eddie, et al., *The Battle of Seattle: The New Challenge to Capitalist Globalization* 2002 (Soft Skull)

Zinn, Howard *SNCC: The New Abolitionists*, Beacon Press 1964

Bibliography:

Buhule, Buhule, and Georgakas eds, *The Encyclopedia of the American Left*, second edition, 1998 (Oxford Press)

Branch, Taylor *Pillar of Fire, America in the King Years 1963-65* 1998 (Touchstone)

Danaher, Kevin et al. *Globalize This!* 2000 (Common Courage Prsss)

Glick, Brian *War At Home: Covert Action Against US Activists and What We Can Do About It* 1989 (South End Press)

Lynd, Staughton, ed *We Are All Leaders, The Alternative Unionism of the Early 1930s* 1996 (University Of Chicago Press)

Manilov, Marianne *Media Alliance How-To Guidebook* 1998 (Media Alliance)

Zinn, Howard *SNCC: The New Abolitionists*, 1964 (Beacon Press)

Baker, Ella J. *Bigger Than A Hamburger* 1964 (self-published)

Thompson, A.C. "Big Brother Was Watching How Bill Clinton Laid the Groundwork for the New Police State" SF Bay Guardian January 18, 2002

San Francisco Industrial Workers of the World *Fire Your Boss!* pamphlet, 1994.

Brown, Jennifer "Over 200 Arrested as Protesters Disrupt Philadelphia." Associated Press, August 1, 2000.

Various Contributors, no editor credited " When Campus Resists" Occupation Press, 1997

Student Nonviolent Coordinating Commitee 1960-1966 www.ibiblio.org/sncc

Welton N., Wolf L. *Global Uprising: Confronting the Tyrannies of the 21st Century. Stories from a New Generation of Activists.* New Society Publishers, 2001

Walt, Kathy, "In Your Face Bootcamp For Activists" Houston Chronicle 05/03/1998

Amon, Michael, "Animal Testing Labs Come Under Fire Again" Washington Square News 09/01/1998

Henderson, Bruce, "Eco-Activism Camp Protesters Teach How to Advocate for Earth" Charlotte Observer Staff Writer 10/01/1998

Brazil, Eric "Ruckus Society chief out on bail" San Francisco Examiner 8/8/2000

Francis X. "Convention Demonstrators Are Held on Very High Bail" New York Times 8/5/2000

Draw your own conclusions here:

Manic D Press Books

Please add $4 to all orders for postage and handling.
Manic D Press • Box 410804 • San Francisco CA 94141 USA
info@manicdpress.com   www.manicdpress.com